Nathan The Wise

Gotthold Ephraim Lessing

Contents

NATHAN THE WISE

A DRAMATIC POEM IN FIVE ACTS

by

Gotthold Ephraim Lessing

INTRODUCTION

Gotthold Ephraim Lessing was born on the 22nd of January, 1729, eldest of ten sons of a pious and learned minister of Camenz in the Oberlausitz, who had two daughters also. As a child Lessing delighted in books, and had knowledge beyond his years when he went to school, in Meissen, at the age of twelve. As a school-boy he read much Greek and Latin that formed no part of the school course; read also the German poets of his time, wrote a "History of Ancient Mathematics," and began a poem of his own on the "Plurality of Worlds." In 1746, at the age of seventeen, Lessing was sent to the University of Leipsic. There he studied with energy, and was attracted strongly by the theatre. His artistic interest in the drama caused him to be put on the free list of the theatre, in exchange for some translations of French pieces. Then he produced, also for the Leipsic stage, many slight pieces of his own, and he had serious thought of turning actor, which excited alarm in the parsonage at Camenz and caused his recall home in January, 1747. It was found, however, that although he could not be trained to follow his father's profession, he had been studying to such good purpose, and developing, in purity of life, such worth of character, that after Easter he was sent back to Leipsic, with leave to transfer his studies from theology to medicine.

Lessing went back, continued to work hard, but still also gave all his leisure to the players. For the debts of some of them he had incautiously become surety, and when the company removed to Vienna, there were left behind them unpaid debts for which young Lessing was answerable. The creditors pressed, and Lessing moved to Wittenberg; but he fell ill, and was made so miserable by pressure for impossible payments, that he resolved to break off his studies, go to Berlin, and begin earning by his pen, his first earnings being for the satisfaction of these Leipsic creditors.

Lessing went first to Berlin to seek his fortune in December, 1748, when he was nineteen years old. He was without money, without decent clothes, and with but one friend in Berlin, Mylius, who was then editing a small journal, the Rudigersche Zeitung. Much correspondence brought him a little money from the overburdened home, and with addition of some small earning from translations, this enabled him to obtain a suit of clothes, in which he might venture to present himself to strangers in his search for fortune. A new venture with Mylius, a quarterly record of the history of the theatre, was not successful; but having charge committed to him of the library part of Mylius's journal, Lessing had an opportunity of showing his great critical power. Gottsched, at Leipsic, was then leader of the war on behalf of classicism in German literature. Lessing fought on the National side, and opposed also the beginning of a new French influence then rising, which was to have its chief apostle in Rousseau.

In 1752 Lessing went back to Wittenberg for another year, that he might complete the work for graduation; graduated in December of that year as Master of Arts, and then returned to his work in Berlin. He worked industriously, not only as critic, but also in translation from the classics, from French, English, and Italian; and he was soon able to send help towards providing education for the youngest of the household of twelve children in the Camenz parsonage. In 1753 he gave himself eight weeks of withdrawal from other work to write, in a garden-house at Potsdam, his tragedy of "Miss Sarah Sampson." It was produced with great success at Frankfort on the Oder, and Lessing's ruling passion for dramatic literature became the stronger for this first experience of what he might be able to achieve. In literature, Frederick the Great cared only for what was French. A National drama, therefore, could not live in Berlin. In the autumn of 1755, Lessing suddenly moved to Leipsic, where an actor whom he had befriended was establishing a theatre. Here he was again abandoning himself to the cause of a National drama, when a rich young gentleman of Leipsic invited his companionship upon a tour in Europe. Terms were settled, and they set out together. They saw much of Holland, and were passing into England, when King Frederick's attack on Saxony recalled the young Leipsiger, and caused breach of what had been a contract for a three years' travelling companionship. In May, 1758, Lessing, aged twenty-nine, returned to his old work in Berlin. Again he translated, edited, criticised. He wrote a tragedy, "Philotas," and began a "Faust." He especially employed his critical power in "Letters upon the Latest Literature," known as his Literatur briefe. Dissertations upon fable, led also to Lessing's "Fables," produced in this period of his life.

In 1760 Lessing was tempted by scarcity of income to serve as a Government secretary at Breslau. He held that office for five years, and then again returned to his old work in Berlin. During the five years in Breslau, Lessing had completed his play of "Minna von Barnhelm," and the greatest of his critical works, "Laocoon," a treatise on the "Boundary Lines of Painting and Poetry." All that he might then have saved from his earnings went to the buying of books and to the relief of the burdens in the Camenz parsonage. At Berlin the office of Royal Librarian became vacant. The claims of Lessing were urged, but Frederick appointed an insignificant Frenchman. In 1767 Lessing was called to aid an unsuccessful attempt to establish a National Theatre in Hamburg.

Other troubles followed. Lessing gave his heart to a widow, Eva Konig, and was betrothed to her. But the involvements of her worldly affairs, and of his, delayed the marriage for six years. To secure fixed income he took a poor office as Librarian at Wolfenbuttel. In his first year at Wolfenbuttel, he wrote his play of "Emilia Galotti." Then came a long-desired journey to Italy; but it came in inconvenient form, for it had to be made with Prince Leopold, of Brunswick, hurriedly, for the sake of money, at the time when Lessing was at last able to marry.

The wife, long waited for, and deeply loved, died at the birth of her first child. This was in January, 1778, when Lessing's age was 49. Very soon afterwards he was attacked by a Pastor Goeze, in Hamburg, and other narrow theologians, for having edited papers that contained an attack on Christianity, which Lessing himself had said that he wished to see answered before he died. The uncharitable bitterness of these attacks, felt by a mind that had been touched to the quick by the deepest of sorrows, helped to the shaping of Lessing's calm, beautiful lesson of charity, this noblest of his plays--"Nathan the Wise." But Lessing's health was shattered, and he survived his wife only three years. He died in 1781, leaving imperishable influence for good upon the minds of men, but so poor in what the world calls wealth, that his funeral had to be paid for by a Duke of Brunswick.

William Taylor, the translator of Lessing's "Nathan the Wise;" was born in 1765, the son of a rich merchant at Norwich, from whose business he was drawn away by his strong bent towards literature. His father yielded to his wishes, after long visits to France and to Germany, in days astir with the new movements of thought, that preceded and followed the French Revolution. He formed a close friendship with Southey, edited for a little time a "Norwich Iris," and in his later years became known especially for his Historic Survey of German Poetry, which included his translations, and among them this of "Nathan the Wise." It was published in 1830, Taylor died in 1836. Thomas Carlyle, in reviewing William Taylor's Survey of German Poetry, said of the author's own translations in it "compared with the average of British translations, they may be pronounced of almost ideal excellence; compared with the best translations extant, for example, the German Shakespeare, Homer, Calderon, they may still be called better than indifferent. One great merit Mr. Taylor has: rigorous adherence to his original; he endeavours at least to copy with all possible fidelity the term of praise, the tone, the very metre, whatever stands written for him."

H. M.

NATHAN THE WISE.

"Introite nam et heic Dii sunt!"--APUD GELLIUM.

DRAMATIS PERSONAE.

SALADIN, the Sultan.
SITTAH, his Sister.
NATHAN, a rich Jew.
RECHA, his adopted Daughter.
DAYA, a Christian Woman dwelling with the Jew a companion to Recha.
CONRADE, a young Templar.
HAFI, a Dervis.
ATHANASIOS, the Patriarch of Palestine.
BONAFIDES, a Friar.
An Emir, sundry Mamalukes, Slaves, &c.

The Scene is at Jerusalem.

ACT I.

SCENE--A Hall in Nathan's House.

NATHAN, in a travelling dress, DAYA meeting him.
DAYA.
'Tis he, 'tis Nathan! Thanks to the Almighty, That you're at last returned.
NATHAN.

Yes, Daya, thanks, That I have reached Jerusalem in safety. But wherefore this AT LAST? Did I intend, Or was it possible to come back sooner? As I was forced to travel, out and in, 'Tis a long hundred leagues to Babylon; And to get in one's debts is no employment, That speeds a traveller.

DAYA.

O Nathan, Nathan, How miserable you had nigh become During this little absence; for your house -

NATHAN,

Well, 'twas on fire; I have already heard it. God grant I may have heard the whole, that chanced!

DAYA.

'Twas on the point of burning to the ground.

NATHAN.

Then we'd have built another, and a better.

DAYA.

True!--But thy Recha too was on the point Of perishing amid the flames.

NATHAN.

Of perishing? My Recha, saidst thou? She? I heard not that. I then should not have needed any house. Upon the point of perishing--perchance She's gone?-- Speak out then--out--torment me not With this suspense.--Come, tell me, tell me all.

DAYA.

Were she no more, from me you would not hear it.

NATHAN.

Why then alarm me?--Recha, O my Recha!

DAYA.

Your Recha? Yours?

NATHAN.

  What if I ever were Doomed to unlearn to call this child, MY child,

DAYA.

Is all you own yours by an equal title?

NATHAN,

Nought by a better. What I else enjoy Nature and Fortune gave--this treasure, Virtue.

DAYA.

How dear you make me pay for all your goodness! - If goodness, exercised with such a view, Deserves the name. -

NATHAN.

With such a view? With what?

DAYA.

My conscience -

NATHAN.

Daya, let me tell you first -

DAYA.

I say, my conscience -

NATHAN.

  What a charming silk I bought for you in Babylon! 'Tis rich, Yet elegantly rich. I almost doubt If I have brought a prettier for Recha.

DAYA.

And what of that--I tell you that my conscience Will no be longer hushed.

NATHAN.

And I have bracelets, And earrings, and a necklace, which will charm you. I chose them at Damascus.

DAYA.

That's your way:- If you can but make presents--but make presents. -

NATHAN.

Take you as freely as I give--and cease.

DAYA.

And cease?--Who questions, Nathan, but that you are Honour and generosity in person; - Yet -

NATHAN.

Yet I'm but a Jew.--That was your meaning.

DAYA.

You better know what was my meaning, Nathan.

NATHAN.

Well, well, no more of this,

DAYA.

I shall be silent; But what of sinful in the eye of heaven Springs out of it--not I, not I could help; It falls upon thy head.

NATHAN.

So let it, Daya. Where is she then? What stays her? Surely, surely, You're not amusing me--And does she know That I'm arrived?

DAYA.

That you yourself must speak to, Terror still vibrates in her every nerve. Her fancy mingles fire with all she thinks of. Asleep, her soul seems busy; but awake, Absent: now less than brute, now more than angel.

NATHAN.

Poor thing! What are we mortals -

DAYA.

As she lay This morning sleeping, all at once she started And cried: "list, list! there come my father's camels!" And then she drooped again upon her pillow And I withdrew--when, lo! you really came. Her thoughts have only been with you--and him.

NATHAN.

And HIM? What him?

DAYA.

  With him, who from the fire Preserved her life,

NATHAN.

  Who was it? Where is he, That saved my Recha for me?

DAYA.

  A young templar, Brought hither captive a few days ago, And pardoned by the Sultan.

NATHAN.

  How, a TEMPLAR Dismissed with life by Saladin. In truth, Not a less miracle was to preserve her, God!--God! -

DAYA.

  Without this man, who risked afresh The Sultan's unexpected boon, we'd lost her.

NATHAN.

Where is he, Daya, where's this noble youth? Do, lead me to his feet. Sure, sure you gave him What treasures I had left you--gave him all, Promised him more--much more?

DAYA.

  How could we?

NATHAN.

  Not?

DAYA.

He came, he went, we know not whence, or whither. Quite unacquainted with the house, unguided But by his ear, he prest through smoke and flame, His mantle spread before him, to the room Whence pierced the shrieks for help; and we began To think him lost--and her; when, all at once, Bursting from flame and smoke, he stood before us, She in his arm upheld. Cold and unmoved By our loud warmth of thanks, he left his booty, Struggled into the crowd, and disappeared.

NATHAN.

But not for ever, Daya, I would hope.

DAYA.

For some days after, underneath you palms, That shade his grave who rose again from death, We saw him wandering up and down. I went, With transport went to thank him. I conjured, Intreated him to visit once again The dear sweet girl he saved, who longed to shed At her preserver's feet the grateful tear -

NATHAN.

Well?

DAYA.

But in vain. Deaf to our warmest prayers, On me he flung such bitter mockery -

NATHAN.

That hence rebuffed -

DAYA.

Oh, no, oh, no, indeed not, Daily I forced myself upon him, daily Afresh encountered his dry taunting speeches. Much I have borne, and would have borne much more: But he of late forbears his lonely walk Under the scattered palms, which stand about Our holy sepulchre: nor have I learnt Where he now is. You seem astonished--thoughtful -

NATHAN.

I was imagining what strange impressions This conduct makes on such a mind as Recha's. Disdained by one whom she must feel compelled To venerate and to esteem so highly. At once attracted and repelled--the combat Between her head and heart must yet endure, Regret, Resentment, in unusual struggle. Neither, perhaps, obtains the upper hand, And busy fancy, meddling in the fray, Weaves wild enthusiasms to her dazzled spirit, Now clothing Passion in the garb of Reason, And Reason now in Passion's--do I err? This last is Recha's fate--Romantic notions -

DAYA.

Aye; but such pious, lovely, sweet, illusions.

NATHAN.

Illusions though.

DAYA.

Yes: and the one, her bosom Clings to most fondly, is, that the brave templar Was but a transient inmate of the earth, A guardian angel, such as from her childhood She loved to fancy kindly hovering round her, Who from his veiling cloud amid the fire Stepped forth in her preserver's form. You smile - Who knows? At least beware of banishing So pleasing an illusion--if deceitful Christian, Jew, Mussulman, agree to own it, And 'tis--at least to her--a dear illusion.

NATHAN.

Also to me. Go, my good Daya, go, See what she's after. Can't I speak with her? Then I'll find out our untamed guardian angel, Bring him to sojourn here awhile among us - We'll pinion his wild wing, when once he's taken.

DAYA.

You undertake too much.

NATHAN.

    And when, my Daya, This sweet illusion yields to sweeter truth, (For to a man a man is ever dearer Than any angel) you must not be angry To see our loved enthusiast exercised.

DAYA.

You are so good--and yet so sly. I'll seek her, But listen,--yes! she's coming of herself.

NATHAN, DAYA, and RECHA.

RECHA.

And you are here, your very self, my father, I thought you'd only sent your voice before you. Where are you then? What mountains, deserts, torrents, Divide us now? You see me, face to face, And do not hasten to embrace your Recha. Poor Recha! she was almost burnt alive, But only--only--almost. Do not shudder! O 'tis a horrid end to die in fire!

NATHAN (embracing her).

My child, my darling child!

RECHA.

    You had to cross The Jordan, Tigris, and Euphrates, and Who knows what rivers else. I used to tremble And quake for you, till the fire came so nigh me; Since then, methinks 'twere comfort, balm, refreshment, To die by water. But you are not drowned - I am not burnt alive.--We will rejoice - We will praise God--the kind good God, who bore thee, Upon the buoyant wings of UNSEEN angels, Across the treacherous stream--the God who bade My angel VISIBLY on his white wing

Athwart the roaring flame -

NATHAN (aside).

  White wing?--oh, aye The broad white fluttering mantle of the templar.

RECHA.

Yes, visibly he bore me through the fire, O'ershadowed by his pinions.--Face to face I've seen an angel, father, my own angel.

NATHAN.

Recha deserves it, and would see in him No fairer form than he beheld in her,

RECHA.

Whom are you flattering, father--tell me now - The angel, or yourself?

NATHAN.

  Yet had a man, A man of those whom Nature daily fashions, Done you this service, he to you had seemed, Had been an angel.

RECHA.

  No, not such a one. Indeed it was a true and real angel. And have not you yourself instructed me How possible it is there may be angels; That God for those who love him can work miracles - And I do love him, father -

NATHAN.

  And he thee; And both for thee, and all like thee, my child, Works daily wonders, from eternity Has wrought them for you.

RECHA.

  That I like to hear.

NATHAN.

Well, and although it sounds quite natural, An every day event, a simple story, That you was by a real templar saved, Is it the less a miracle? The greatest Of all is this, that true and real wonders Should happen so perpetually, so daily. Without this universal miracle A thinking man had scarcely called those such, Which only children, Recha, ought to name so, Who love to gape and stare at the unusual And hunt for novelty -

DAYA.

  Why will you then With such vain subtleties, confuse her brain Already overheated?

NATHAN.

Let me manage. - And is it not enough then for my Recha To owe her preservation to a man, Whom no small miracle preserved himself. For whoe'er heard before that Saladin Let go a templar; that a templar wished it, Hoped it, or for his ransom offered more Than taunts, his leathern sword-belt, or his dagger?

RECHA.

That makes for me; these are so many reasons He was no real knight, but only seemed it. If in Jerusalem no captive templar, Appears alive, or freely wanders round, How could I find one, in the night, to save me?

NATHAN.

Ingenious! dextrous! Daya, come in aid. It was from you I learnt he was a prisoner; Doubtless you know still more about him, speak.

DAYA.

'Tis but report indeed, but it is said That Saladin bestowed upon this youth His gracious pardon for the strong resemblance He bore a favourite brother--dead, I think These twenty years--his name, I know it not - He fell, I don't know where-- and all the story Sounds so incredible, that very likely The whole is mere invention, talk, romance.

NATHAN.

And why incredible? Would you reject This story, tho' indeed, it's often done, To fix on something more incredible, And give that faith? Why should not Saladin, Who loves so singularly all his kindred, Have loved in early youth with warmer fondness A brother now no more. Do we not see Faces alike, and is an old impression Therefore a lost one? Do resembling features Not call up like emotions. Where's th' incredible? Surely, sage Daya, this can be to thee No miracle, or do THY wonders only Demand--I should have said DESERVE belief?

DAYA.

You're on the bite.

NATHAN.

Were you quite fair with me? Yet even so, my Recha, thy escape Remains a wonder, only possible To Him, who of the proud pursuits of princes Makes sport-- or if not sport--at least delights To head and manage them by slender threads.

RECHA.

If I do err, it is not wilfully, My father.

NATHAN.

No, you have been always docile. See now, a forehead vaulted thus, or thus - A nose bow'd one way rather than another - Eye-brows with straiter, or with sharper curve - A line, a mole, a wrinkle, a mere nothing I' th' countenance of an European savage - And thou--art saved, in Asia, from the fire. Ask ye for signs and wonders after that? What need of calling angels into play?

DAYA.

But Nathan, where's the harm, if I may speak, Of fancying one's self by an angel saved, Rather than by a man? Methinks it brings us Just so much the nearer the incomprehensive First cause of preservation.

NATHAN.

Pride, rank pride! The iron pot would with a silver prong Be lifted from the furnace--to imagine Itself a silver vase. Paha! Where's the harm? Thou askest. Where's the good? I might reply. For thy IT BRINGS US NEARER TO THE GOD-HEAD Is nonsense, Daya, if not blasphemy. But it does harm: yes, yes, it does indeed. Attend now. To the being, who preserved you, Be he an angel or a man, you both, And thou especially wouldst gladly show Substantial services in just requital. Now to an angel what great services Have ye the power to do? To sing his praise - Melt in transporting contemplation o'er him - Fast on his holiday--and squander alms - What nothingness of use! To me at least It seems your neighbour gains much more than he By all this pious glow. Not by your fasting Is he made fat; not by your squandering, rich; Nor by your transports is his glory exalted; Nor by your faith his might. But to a man -

DAYA.

Why yes; a man indeed had furnished us With more occasions to be useful to him. God knows how readily we should have seized them. But then he would have nothing--wanted nothing - Was in himself wrapped up, and self-sufficient, As angels are.

RECHA.

And when at last he vanished -

NATHAN.

Vanished? How vanished? Underneath the palms Escaped your view, and has returned no more. Or have you really sought for him elsewhere?

DAYA.
No, that indeed we've not.
NATHAN.
   Not, Daya, not? See it does harm, hard-hearted, cold enthusiasts, What if this angel on a bed of illness -
RECHA.
Illness?
DAYA.
   Ill! sure he is not.
RECHA.
   A cold shudder Creeps over me; O Daya, feel my forehead, It was so warm, 'tis now as chill as ice.
NATHAN.
He is a Frank, unused to this hot climate, Is young, and to the labours of his calling, To fasting, watching, quite unused -
RECHA.
   Ill--ill!
DAYA.
Thy father only means 'twere possible.
NATHAN.
And there he lies, without a friend, or money To buy him friends -
RECHA.
   Alas! my father.
NATHAN.
   Lies Without advice, attendance, converse, pity, The prey of agony, of death -

RECHA.
   Where--where?
NATHAN.
He, who, for one he never knew, or saw - It is enough for him he is a man - Plunged into fire.
DAYA.
   O Nathan, Nathan, spare her.

NATHAN.

Who cared not to know aught of her he saved, Declined her presence to escape her thanks -

DAYA.

Do, spare her!

NATHAN.

Did not wish to see her more Unless it were a second time to save her - Enough for him he is a man -

DAYA.

Stop, look!

NATHAN.

He--he, in death, has nothing to console him, But the remembrance of this deed.

DAYA.

You kill her!

NATHAN.

And you kill him--or might have done at least - Recha 'tis medicine I give, not poison. He lives--come to thyself--may not be ill - Not even ill -

RECHA.

Surely not dead, not dead.

NATHAN.

Dead surely not--for God rewards the good Done here below, here too. Go; but remember How easier far devout enthusiasm is Than a good action; and how willingly Our indolence takes up with pious rapture, Tho' at the time unconscious of its end, Only to save the toil of useful deeds.

RECHA.

Oh never leave again thy child alone! - But can he not be only gone a journey?

NATHAN.

Yes, very likely. There's a Mussulman Numbering with curious eye my laden camels, Do you know who he is?

DAYA.

Oh, your old dervis.

NATHAN.

Who--who?

DAYA.

  Your chess companion.

NATHAN.

    That, Al-Hafi?

DAYA.

And now the treasurer of Saladin.

NATHAN.

Al-Hafi? Are you dreaming? How was this? In fact it is so. He seems coming hither. In with you quick.--What now am I to hear?

NATHAN and HAFI.

HAFI.

Aye, lift thine eyes in wonder.

NATHAN.

  Is it you? A dervis so magnificent! -

HAFI.

  Why not? Can nothing then be made out of a dervis?

NATHAN.

Yes, surely; but I have been wont to think A dervis, that's to say a thorough dervis, Will allow nothing to be made of him.

HAFI.

May-be 'tis true that I'm no thorough dervis; But by the prophet, when we must -

NATHAN.

  Must, Hafi? Needs must--belongs to no man: and a dervis -

HAFI.

When he is much besought, and thinks it right, A dervis must.

NATHAN.

  Well spoken, by our God! Embrace me, man, you're still, I trust, my friend.

HAFI.

Why not ask first what has been made of me?

NATHAN.

Ask climbers to look back!
HAFI.

And may I not Have grown to such a creature in the state That my old friend-ship is no longer welcome?

NATHAN.

If you still bear your dervis-heart about you I'll run the risk of that. Th' official robe Is but your cloak.

HAFI.

A cloak, that claims some honour. What think'st thou? At a court of thine how great Had been Al-Hafi?

NATHAN.

Nothing but a dervis. If more, perhaps--what shall I say--my cook.

HAFI.

In order to unlearn my native trade. Thy cook--why not thy butler too? The Sultan, He knows me better, I'm his treasurer.

NATHAN.

You, you?

HAFI.

Mistake not--of the lesser purse - His father manages the greater still - The purser of his household.

NATHAN.

That's not small.

HAFI.

'Tis larger than thou think'st; for every beggar Is of his household.

NATHAN.

He's so much their foe -

HAFI.

That he'd fain root them out--with food and raiment - Tho' he turn beggar in the enterprize.

NATHAN.

Bravo, I meant so.

HAFI.

And he's almost such. His treasury is every day, ere sun-set, Poorer than empty; and how high so e'er Flows in the morning tide, 'tis ebb by noon.

NATHAN.

Because it circulates through such canals As can be neither stopped, nor filled.

HAFI.

   Thou hast it.

NATHAN.

I know it well.

HAFI.

   Nathan, 'tis woeful doing When kings are vultures amid caresses: But when they're caresses amid the vultures 'Tis ten times worse.

NATHAN.

   No, dervis, no, no, no.

HAFI.

Thou mayst well talk so. Now then, let me hear What wouldst thou give me to resign my office?

NATHAN.

What does it bring you in?

HAFI.

   To me, not much; But thee, it might indeed enrich: for when, As often happens, money is at ebb, Thou couldst unlock thy sluices, make advances, And take in form of interest all thou wilt.

NATHAN.

And interest upon interest of the interest -

HAFI.

Certainly.

NATHAN.

   Till my capital becomes All interest.

HAFI.

How--that does not take with thee? Then write a finis to our book of friendship; For I have reckoned on thee.

NATHAN.

   How so, Hafi?

HAFI.

That thou wouldst help me to go thro' my office With credit, grant me open chest with thee - Dost shake thy head?

NATHAN.

    Let's understand each other. Here's a distinction to be made. To you, To dervis Hafi, all I have is open; But to the defterdar of Saladin, To that Al-Hafi -

HAFI.

    Spoken like thyself! Thou hast been ever no less kind than cautious. The two Al-Hafis thou distinguishest Shall soon be parted. See this coat of honour, Which Saladin bestowed--before 'tis worn To rags, and suited to a dervis' back, - Will in Jerusalem hang upon the hook; While I along the Ganges scorching strand, Amid my teachers shall be wandering barefoot.

NATHAN.

That's like you.

HAFI.

    Or be playing chess among them.

NATHAN.

Your sovereign good.

HAFI.

    What dost thou think seduced me. The wish of having not to beg in future - The pride of acting the rich man to beggars - Would these have metamorphosed a rich beggar So suddenly into a poor rich man?

NATHAN.

No, I think not.

HAFI.

    A sillier, sillier weakness, For the first time my vanity was tempter, Flattered by Saladin's good-hearted notion -

NATHAN.

Which was?

HAFI.

    That all a beggar's wants are only Known to a beggar: such alone can tell How to relieve them usefully and wisely. "Thy predecessor was too cold for me, (He said) and when he gave, he gave unkindly; Informed himself with too precautious strictness Concerning the receiver, not content To leant the want, unless he knew its cause, And measuring out by that his niggard bounty. Thou wilt not thus bestow. So harshly kind Shall Saladin not seem in thee. Thou art not Like the choked pipe, whence sullied and by spurts Flow the pure waters it absorbs in silence. Al-Hafi thinks and feels like me." So nicely The fowler whistled, that at last the quail Ran to his net. Cheated, and by a cheat -

NATHAN.

Tush! dervis, gently.

HAFI.

What! and is't not cheating, Thus to oppress mankind by hundred thousands, To squeeze, grind, plunder, butcher, and torment, And act philanthropy to individuals? - Not cheating--thus to ape from the Most High The bounty, which alike on mead and desert, Upon the just and the unrighteous, falls In sunshine or in showers, and not possess The never-empty hand of the Most High? - Not cheating -

NATHAN.

Cease!

HAFI.

Of my own cheating sure It is allowed to speak. Were it not cheating To look for the fair side of these impostures, In order, under colour of its fairness, To gain advantage from them--ha?

NATHAN.

Al-Hafi, Go to your desert quickly. Among men I fear you'll soon unlearn to be a man.

HAFI.

And so do I--farewell.

NATHAN.

What, so abruptly? Stay, stay, Al-Hafi; has the desert wings? Man, 'twill not run away, I warrant you - Hear, hear, I want you--want to talk with you - He's gone. I could have liked to question him About our templar. He will likely know him.

NATHAN and DAYA. DAYA (bursting in).

O Nathan, Nathan!

NATHAN.

Well, what now?

DAYA.

He's there. He shows himself again.

NATHAN.

Who, Daya, who?

DAYA.

He! he!

NATHAN.

When cannot He be seen? Indeed Your He is only one; that should not be, Were he an angel even.

DAYA.

'Neath the palms He wanders up and down, and gathers dates.

NATHAN.

And eats?--and as a templar?

DAYA.

How you tease us! Her eager eye espied him long ago, While he scarce gleamed between the further stems, And follows him most punctually. Go, She begs, conjures you, go without delay; And from the window will make signs to you Which way his rovings bend. Do, do make haste.

NATHAN.

What! thus, as I alighted from my camel, Would that be decent? Swift, do you accost him, Tell him of my return. I do not doubt, His delicacy in the master's absence Forbore my house; but gladly will accept The father's invitation. Say, I ask him, Most heartily request him -

DAYA.

All in vain! In short, he will not visit any Jew.

NATHAN.

Then do thy best endeavours to detain him, Or with thine eyes to watch his further haunt, Till I rejoin you. I shall not be long.

SCENE--A Place of Palms.

The TEMPLAR walking to and fro, a FRIAR following him at some distance, as if desirous of addressing him.

TEMPLAR.

This fellow does not follow me for pastime. How skaunt he eyes his hands! Well, my good brother - Perhaps I should say, father; ought I not?

FRIAR.

No--brother--a lay-brother at your service.

TEMPLAR.

Well, brother, then; if I myself had something - But--but, by God, I've noth-ing.

FRIAR.

   Thanks the same; And God reward your purpose thousand-fold! The will, and not the deed, makes up the giver. Nor was I sent to follow you for alms -

TEMPLAR.

Sent then?

FRIAR.

   Yes, from the monastery.

TEMPLAR.

   Where I was just now in hopes of coming in For pilgrims' fare.

FRIAR.

   They were already at table: But if it suit with you to turn directly -

TEMPLAR.

Why so? 'Tis true, I have not tasted meat This long time. What of that? The dates are ripe.

FRIAR.

O with that fruit go cautiously to work. Too much of it is hurtful, sours the humours, Makes the blood melancholy.

TEMPLAR.

   And if I Choose to be melancholy--For this warning You were not sent to follow me, I ween.

FRIAR.

Oh, no: I only was to ask about you, And feel your pulse a little.

TEMPLAR.

   And you tell me Of that yourself?

FRIAR.

Why not?

TEMPLAR.

A deep one! troth: And has your cloister more such?

FRIAR.

I can't say. Obedience is our bounden duty.

TEMPLAR.

So - And you obey without much scrupulous questioning?

FRIAR.

Were it obedience else, good sir?

TEMPLAR.

How is it The simple mind is ever in the right? May you inform me who it is that wishes To know more of me? 'Tis not you yourself, I dare be sworn.

FRIAR.

Would it become me, sir, Or benefit me?

TEMPLAR.

Whom can it become, Whom can it benefit, to be so curious?

FRIAR.

The patriarch, I presume--'twas he that sent me.

TEMPLAR.

The patriarch? Knows he not my badge, the cross Of red on the white mantle?

FRIAR.

Can I say?

TEMPLAR.

Well, brother, well! I am a templar, taken Prisoner at Tebnin, whose exalted fortress, Just as the truce expired, we sought to climb, In order to push forward next to Sidon. I was the twentieth captive, but the only Pardoned by Saladin--with this, the patriarch Knows all, or more than his occasions ask.

FRIAR.

And yet no more than he already knows, I think. But why alone of all the captives Thou hast been spared, he fain would learn -

TEMPLAR.

Can I Myself tell that? Already, with bare neck, I kneeled upon my mantle, and awaited The blow--when Saladin with steadfast eye Fixed me, sprang nearer to me, made a sign - I was upraised, unbound, about to thank him - And saw his eye in tears. Both stand in silence. He goes. I stay. How all this hangs together, Thy patriarch may unriddle.

FRIAR.

He concludes, That God preserved you for some mighty deed.

TEMPLAR.

Some mighty deed? To save out of the fire A Jewish girl--to usher curious pilgrims About Mount Sinai--to -

FRIAR.

The time may come - And this is no such trifle--but perhaps The patriarch meditates a weightier office.

TEMPLAR.

Think you so, brother? Has he hinted aught?

FRIAR.

Why, yes; I was to sift you out a little, And hear if you were one to -

TEMPLAR.

Well--to what? I'm curious to observe how this man sifts.

FRIAR.

The shortest way will be to tell you plainly What are the patriarch's wishes.

TEMPLAR.

And they are -

FRIAR.

To send a letter by your hand.

TEMPLAR.

By me? I am no carrier. And were that an office More meritorious than to save from burning A Jewish maid?

FRIAR.

So it should seem; must seem - For, says the patriarch, to all Christendom This letter is of import; and to bear it Safe to its destination, says the patriarch, God will reward with a peculiar crown In heaven; and of this crown, the patriarch says, No one is worthier than you -

TEMPLAR.

Than I?
FRIAR.
For none so able, and so fit to earn This crown, the patriarch says, as you.
TEMPLAR.
   As I?
FRIAR.
The patriarch here is free, can look about him, And knows, he says, how cities may be stormed, And how defended; knows, he says, the strengths And weaknesses of Saladin's new bulwark, And of the inner rampart last thrown up; And to the warriors of the Lord, he says, Could clearly point them out; -
TEMPLAR.
   And can I know Exactly the contents of this same letter?
FRIAR.
Why, that I don't pretend to vouch exactly - 'Tis to King Philip: and our patriarch - I often wonder how this holy man, Who lives so wholly to his God and heaven, Can stoop to be so well informed about Whatever passes here--'Tis a hard task!
TEMPLAR.
Well--and your patriarch -
FRIAR.
   Knows, with great precision, And from sure hands, how, when, and with what force, And in which quarter, Saladin, in case The war breaks out afresh, will take the field.
TEMPLAR.
He knows that?
FRIAR.
   Yes; and would acquaint King Philip, That he may better calculate, if really The danger be so great as to require Him to renew at all events the truce So bravely broken by your body.
TEMPLAR.
   So? This is a patriarch indeed! He wants No common messenger; he wants a spy. Go tell your patriarch, brother, I am not, As far as you can sift, the man to suit him. I still esteem myself a prisoner, and A templar's only calling is to fight, And

not to ferret out intelligence.

FRIAR.

That's much as I supposed, and, to speak plainly, Not to be blamed. The best is yet behind. The patriarch has made out the very fortress, Its name, and strength, and site on Libanon, Wherein the mighty sums are now concealed, With which the prudent father of the sultan Provides the cost of war, and pays the army. He knows that Saladin, from time to time, Goes to this fortress, through by-ways and passe With few attendants.

TEMPLAR.

Well -

FRIAR.

How easy 'twere To seize his person in these expeditions, And make an end of all! You shudder, sir - Two Maronites, who fear the Lord, have offer To share the danger of the enterprise, Under a proper leader.

TEMPLAR.

And the patriarch Had cast his eye on me for this brave office?

FRIAR.

He thinks King Philip might from Ptolemais Best second such a deed.

TEMPLAR.

On me? on me? Have you not heard then, just now heard, the favour Which I received from Saladin?

FRIAR.

Oh, yes!

TEMPLAR.

And yet?

FRIAR.

The patriarch thinks--that's mighty well - God, and the order's interest -

TEMPLAR.

Alter nothing, Command no villainies.

FRIAR.

No, that indeed not; But what is villainy in human eyes May in the sight of God, the patriarch thinks, Not be -

TEMPLAR.

I owe my life to Saladin, And might take his?
FRIAR.

That--fie! But Saladin, The patriarch thinks, is yet the common foe Of Christendom, and cannot earn a right To be your friend.
TEMPLAR.

My friend--because I will not Behave like an ungrateful scoundrel to him.
FRIAR.

Yet gratitude, the patriarch thinks, is not A debt before the eye of God or man, Unless for our own sakes the benefit Had been conferred; and, it has been reported, The patriarch understands that Saladin Preserved your life merely because your voice, Your air, or features, raised a recollection Of his lost brother.
TEMPLAR.

He knows this? and yet - If it were sure, I should--ah, Saladin! How! and shall nature then have formed in me A single feature in thy brother's likeness, With nothing in my soul to answer to it? Or what does correspond shall I suppress To please a patriarch? So thou dost not cheat us, Nature--and so not contradict Thyself, Kind God of all.--Go, brother, go away: Do not stir up my anger.
FRIAR.

I withdraw More gladly than I came. We cloister-folk Are forced to vow obedience to superiors. [Goes
TEMPLAR and DAYA. DAYA.

The monk, methinks, left him in no good mood: But I must risk my message.
TEMPLAR.

Better still The proverb says that monks and women are The devil's clutches; and I'm tossed to-day From one to th' other.
DAYA.

Whom do I behold? - Thank God! I see you, noble knight, once more. Where have you lurked this long, long space? You've not Been ill?
TEMPLAR.

No.
DAYA.

Well, then?
TEMPLAR.

Yes.
DAYA.
   We've all been anxious Lest something ailed you.
TEMPLAR.
   So?
DAYA.
   Have you been journeying?
TEMPLAR.
Hit off!
DAYA.
   How long returned?
TEMPLAR.
   Since yesterday.
DAYA.
Our Recha's father too is just returned, And now may Recha hope at last -
TEMPLAR.
   For what?
DAYA.

For what she often has requested of you. Her father pressingly invites your visit. He now arrives from Babylon, with twenty High-laden camels, brings the curious drugs, And precious stones, and stuffs, he has collected From Syria, Persia, India, even China.
TEMPLAR.
I am no chap.
DAYA.

   His nation honours him, As if he were a prince, and yet to hear him Called the WISE Nathan by them, not the RICH, Has often made me wonder.
TEMPLAR.
   To his nation Are RICH and WISE perhaps of equal import.
DAYA.

But above all he should be called the GOOD. You can't imagine how much goodness dwells Within him. Since he has been told the service You rendered to his Recha, there is nothing That he would grudge you.

TEMPLAR.

Aye?

DAYA.

Do--see him, try him.

TEMPLAR.

A burst of feeling soon is at an end.

DAYA.

And do you think that I, were he less kind, Less bountiful, had housed with him so long: That I don't feel my value as a Christian: For 'twas not o'er my cradle said, or sung, That I to Palestina should pursue My husband's steps, only to educate A Jewess. My husband was a noble page In Emperor Frederic's army.

TEMPLAR.

And by birth A Switzer, who obtained the gracious honour Of drowning in one river with his master. Woman, how often you have told me this! Will you ne'er leave off persecuting me?

DAYA.

My Jesus! persecute -

TEMPLAR.

Aye, persecute. Observe then, I henceforward will not see, Not hear you, nor be minded of a deed Over and over, which I did unthinking, And which, when thought about, I wonder at. I wish not to repent it; but, remember, Should the like accident occur again, 'Twill be your fault if I proceed more coolly, Ask a few questions, and let burn what's burning.

DAYA.

My God forbid!

TEMPLAR.

From this day forth, good woman, Do me at least the favour not to know me: I beg it of you; and don't send the father. A Jew's a Jew, and I am rude and bearish. The image of the maid is quite erased Out of my soul--if it was ever there -

DAYA.

But yours remains with her.

TEMPLAR.

Why so--what then - Wherefore give harbour to it? -

DAYA.

  Who knows wherefore? Men are not always what they seem to be.

TEMPLAR.

They're seldom better than they seem to be.

DAYA.

Ben't in this hurry.

TEMPLAR.

  Pray, forbear to make These palm-trees odious. I have loved to walk here.

DAYA.

Farewell then, bear. Yet I must track the savage.

ACT II.

SCENE--The Sultan's Palace.--An outer room of Sittah's apartment.

SALADIN and SITTAH, playing chess.
SITTAH.
Wherefore so absent, brother? How you play!
SALADIN.
Not well? I thought -
SITTAH.
   Yes; very well for me, Take back that move.
SALADIN.
   Why?
SITTAH.
    Don't you see the knight Becomes exposed?
SALADIN.
   'Tis true: then so.
SITTAH.
     And so I take the pawn.
SALADIN.
   That's true again. Then, check!
SITTAH.
That cannot help you. When my king is castled All will be safe.
SALADIN.
   But out of my dilemma 'Tis not so easy to escape unhurt. Well, you must have the knight.
   SITTAH.

I will not have him, I pass him by.
SALADIN.

In that, there's no forbearance: The place is better than the piece.
SITTAH.

Maybe.
SALADIN.

Beware you reckon not without your host: This stroke you did not think of.
SITTAH.

No, indeed; I did not think you tired of your queen.
SALADIN.

My queen?
SITTAH.

Well, well! I find that I to-day Shall earn a thousand dinars to an asper.
SALADIN.

How so, my sister?
SITTAH.

Play the ignorant - As if it were not purposely thou losest. I find not my account in 't; for, besides That such a game yields very little pastime, When have I not, by losing, won with thee? When hast thou not, by way of comfort to me For my lost game, presented twice the stake?
SALADIN.

So that it may have been on purpose, sister, That thou hast lost at times.
SITTAH.

At least, my brother's Great liberality may be one cause Why I improve no faster.
SALADIN.

We forget The game before us: lot us make an end of it.
SITTAH.

I move--so--now then--check! and check again!
SALADIN.

This countercheck I wasn't aware of, Sittah; My queen must fall the sacrifice.
SITTAH.

Let's see - Could it be helped?

SALADIN.

No, no, take off the queen! That is a piece which never thrives with me.

SITTAH.

Only that piece?

SALADIN.

Off with it! I shan't miss it. Thus I guard all again.

SITTAH.

How civilly We should behave to queens, my brother's lessons Have taught me but too well.

SALADIN.

Take her, or not, I stir the piece no more.

SITTAH.

Why should I take her? Check!

SALADIN.

Go on.

SITTAH.

Check! -

SALADIN.

And check-mate?

SITTAH.

Hold! not yet. You may advance the knight, and ward the danger, Or as you will--it is all one.

SALADIN.

It is so. You are the winner, and Al-Hafi pays. Let him be called. Sittah, you was not wrong; I seem to recollect I was unmindful - A little absent. One isn't always willing To dwell upon some shapeless bits of wood Coupled with no idea. Yet the Imam, When I play with him, bends with such abstraction - The loser seeks excuses. Sittah, 'twas not The shapeless men, and the unmeaning squares, That made me heedless--your dexterity, Your calm sharp eye.

SITTAH.

And what of that, good brother, Is that to be th' excuse for your defeat? Enough--you played more absently than I.

SALADIN.

Than you! What dwells upon your mind, my Sittah? Not your own cares, I doubt -

SITTAH.

O Saladin, When shall we play again so constantly?

SALADIN.

An interruption will but whet our zeal. You think of the campaign. Well, let it come. It was not I who first unsheathed the sword. I would have willingly prolonged the truce, And willingly have knit a closer bond, A lasting one--have given to my Sittah A husband worthy of her, Richard's brother.

SITTAH.

You love to talk of Richard.

SALADIN.

Richard's sister Might then have been allotted to our Melek. O what a house that would have formed--the first - The best--and what is more--of earth the happiest! You know I am not loth to praise myself; Why should I?--Of my friends am I not worthy? O we had then led lives!

SITTAH.

A pretty dream. It makes me smile. You do not know the Christians. You will not know them. 'Tis this people's pride Not to be men, but to be Christians. Even What of humane their Founder felt, and taught, And left to savour their found superstition, They value not because it is humane, Lovely, and good for man; they only prize it Because 'twas Christ who taught it, Christ who did it. 'Tis well for them He was so good a man: Well that they take His goodness all for granted, And in His virtues put their trust. His virtues - 'Tis not His virtues, but His name alone They wish to thrust upon us--'Tis His name Which they desire should overspread the world, Should swallow up the name of all good men, And put the best to shame. 'Tis His mere name They care for -

SALADIN.

Else, my Sittah, as thou sayst, They would not have required that thou, and Melek, Should be called Christians, ere you might be suffered To feel for Christians conjugal affection.

SITTAH.

As if from Christians only, and as Christians, That love could be expected which our Maker In man and woman for each other planted.

SALADIN.

The Christians do believe such idle notions, They well might fancy this: and yet thou errest. The templars, not the Christians, are in fault. 'Tis not as Christians, but as templars, that They thwart my purpose. They alone prevent it. They will on no account evacuate Acca, Which was to be the dower of Richard's sister, And, lest their order suffer, use this cant - Bring into play the nonsense of the monk - And scarcely would await the truce's end To fall upon us. Go on so--go on, To me you're welcome, sirs. Would all things else Went but as right!

SITTAH.

What else should trouble thee, If this do not?

SALADIN.

Why, that which ever has. I've been on Libanon, and seen our father. He's full of care.

SITTAH.

Alas!

SALADIN.

He can't make shift, Straitened on all sides, put off, disappointed; Nothing comes in.

SITTAH.

What fails him, Saladin?

SALADIN.

What? but the thing I scarcely deign to name, Which, when I have it, so superfluous seems, And, when I have it not, so necessary. Where is Al-Hafi then--this fatal money - O welcome, Hafi!

HAFI, SALADIN, and SITTAH.

HAFI.

I suppose the gold From Egypt is arrived.

SALADIN.

Hast tidings of it?

HAFI.

I? no, not I. I thought to have ta'en it here.

SALADIN.

To Sittah pay a thousand dinars.
HAFI.

Pay? And not receive--that's something less than nothing. To Sittah and again to Sittah--and Once more for loss at chess? Is this your game?
SITTAH.
Dost grudge me my good fortune?
HAFI (examining the board).

Grudge! you know -
SITTAH (making signs to Hafi).
Hush, Hafi, hush!
HAFI.

And were the white men yours? You gave the check?
SITTAH.

'Tis well he does not hear.
HAFI.
And he to move?
SITTAH (approaching Hafi).

Say then aloud that I Shall have my money.
HAFI (still considering the game).

Yes, yes! you shall have it - As you have always had it.
SITTAH.

Are you crazy?
HAFI.
The game is not decided; Saladin, You have not lost.
SALADIN (scarcely hearkening).

Well, well!--pay, pay.
HAFI.

Pay, pay - There stands your queen.
SALADIN (still walking about).

It boots not, she is useless.
SITTAH (low to Hafi).
Do say that I may send and fetch the gold.
HAFI.

Aye, aye, as usual--But although the queen Be useless, you are by no means check-mate.

SALADIN (dashes down the board).

I am. I will then -

HAFI.

So! small pains, small gains; As got, so spent.

SALADIN (to Sittah).

What is he muttering there?

SITTAH (to Saladin, winking meanwhile to Hafi).

You know him well, and his unyielding way. He chooses to be prayed to--maybe he's envious -

SALADIN.

No, not of thee, not of my sister, surely. What do I hear, Al-Hafi, are you envious?

HAFI.

Perhaps. I'd rather have her head than mine, Or her heart either.

SITTAH.

Ne'ertheless, my brother, He pays me right, and will again to-day. Let him alone. There, go away, Al-Hafi; I'll send and fetch my dinars.

HAFI.

No, I will not; I will not act this farce a moment longer: He shall, must know it.

SALADIN.

Who? what?

SITTAH.

O Al-Hafi, Is this thy promise, this thy keeping word?

HAFI.

How could I think it was to go so far?

SALADIN.

Well, what am I to know?

SITTAH.

I pray thee, Hafi, Be more discreet.

SALADIN.

That's very singular. And what can Sittah then so earnestly, So warmly have to sue for from a stranger, A dervis, rather than from me, her brother? Al-Hafi, I command. Dervis, speak out.

SITTAH.

Let not a trifle, brother, touch you nearer Than is becoming. You know I have often Won the same sum of you at chess, and, as I have not just at present need of money, I've left the sum at rest in Hafi's chest, Which is not over-full; and thus the stakes Are not yet taken out--but, never fear, It is not my intention to bestow them On thee, or Hafi.

HAFI.

 Were it only this -

SITTAH.

Some more such trifles are perhaps unclaimed; My own allowance, which you set apart, Has lain some months untouched.

HAFI.

 Nor is that all -

SALADIN.

Nor yet--speak then!

HAFI.

 Since we have been expecting The treasure out of Egypt, she not only -

SITTAH.

Why listen to him?

HAFI.

 Has not had an asper; -

SALADIN.

Good creature--but has been advancing to thee -

HAFI.

Has at her sole expense maintained thy state.

SALADIN (embracing her).

My sister--ah!

SITTAH.

 And who but you, my brother, Could make me rich enough to have the power?

HAFI.
And in a little time again will leave thee Poor as himself.
SALADIN.
I, poor--her brother, poor? When had I more, when less than at this instant? A cloak, a horse, a sabre, and a God! - What need I else? With them what can be wanting? And yet, Al-Hafi, I could quarrel with thee For this.
SITTAH.
A truce to that, my brother. Were it As easy to remove our father's cares!
SALADIN.
Ah! now my joy thou hast at once abated: To me there is, there can be, nothing wanting; But--but to him--and, in him, to us all. What shall I do? From Egypt maybe nothing Will come this long time. Why--God only knows. We hear of no stir. To reduce, to spare, I am quite willing for myself to stoop to, Were it myself, and only I, should suffer - But what can that avail? A cloak, a horse, A sword I ne'er can want;--as to my God, He is not to be bought; He asks but little, Only my heart. I had relied, Al-Hafi, Upon a surplus in my chest.
HAFI.
A surplus? And tell me, would you not have had me impaled, Or hanged at least, if you had found me out In hoarding up a surplus? Deficits - Those one may venture on.
SALADIN.
Well, but how next? Could you have found out no one where to borrow Unless of Sittah?
SITTAH.
And would I have borne To see the preference given to another? I still lay claim to it. I am not as yet Entirely bare.
SALADIN.
Not yet entirely--This Was wanting still. Go, turn thyself about; Take where, and as, thou canst; be quick, Al-Hafi. Borrow on promise, contract, anyhow; But heed me--not of those I have enriched - To borrow there might seem to ask it back. Go to the covetous. They'll gladliest lend - They know how well their money thrives with me -
HAFI.

I know none such.

SITTAH.

I recollect just now I heard, Al-Hafi, of thy friend's return.

HAFI (startled).

Friend--friend of mine--and who should that be?

SITTAH.

Who? Thy vaunted Jew!

HAFI.

A Jew, and praised by me?

SITTAH.

To whom his God (I think I still retain Thy own expression used concerning him) To whom, of all the good things of this world, His God in full abundance has bestowed The greatest and the least.

HAFI.

What could I mean When I said so?

SITTAH.

The least of good things, riches; The greatest, wisdom.

HAFI.

How--and of a Jew Could I say that?

SITTAH.

Didst thou not--of thy Nathan?

HAFI.

Hi ho! of him--of Nathan? At that moment He did not come across me. But, in fact, He is at length come home; and, I suppose, Is not ill off. His people used to call him The wise--also the rich.

SITTAH.

The rich he's named Now more than ever. The whole town resounds With news of jewels, costly stuffs, and stores, That he brings back.

HAFI.

Is he the rich again - He'll be, no fear of it, once more the wise.

SITTAH.

What thinkst thou, Hafi, of a call on him?

HAFI.

On him--sure not to borrow--why, you know him - He lend? Therein his very wisdom lies, That he lends no one.

SITTAH.

Formerly thon gav'st A very different picture of this Nathan.

HAFI.

In case of need he'll lend you merchandise, But money, money, never. He's a Jew, There are but few such! he has understanding, Knows life, plays chess; but is in bad notorious Above his brethren, as he is in good. On him rely not. To the poor indeed He vies perhaps with Saladin in giving: Though he distributes less, he gives as freely, As silently, as nobly, to Jew, Christian, Mahometan, or Parsee--'tis all one.

SITTAH.

And such a man should be -

SALADIN.

How comes it then I never heard of him?

SITTAH.

Should be unwilling To lend to Saladin, who wants for others, Not for himself.

HAFI.

Aye, there peeps out the Jew, The ordinary Jew. Believe me, prince, He's jealous, really envious of your giving. To earn God's favour seems his very business. He lends not that he may always have to give. The law commandeth mercy, not compliance: And thus for mercy's sake he's uncomplying. 'Tis true, I am not now on the best terms With Nathan, but I must entreat you, think not That therefore I would do injustice to him. He's good in everything, but not in that - Only in that. I'll knock at other doors. I just have recollected an old Moor, Who's rich and covetous--I go--I go.

SITTAH.

Why in such hurry, Hafi?

SALADIN.

Let him go.

SALADIN and SITTAH.

SITTAH.

He hastens like a man who would escape me; Why so? Was he indeed deceived in Nathan, Or does he play upon us?

SALADIN.

Can I guess? I scarcely know of whom you have been talking, And hear to-day, for the first time, of Nathan.

SITTAH.

Is't possible the man were hid from thee, Of whom 'tis said, he has found out the tombs Of Solomon and David, knows the word That lifts their marble lids, and thence obtains The golden oil that feeds his shining pomp?

SALADIN.

Were this man's wealth by miracle created, 'Tis not at David's tomb, or Solomon's, That 'twould be wrought. Not virtuous men lie there.

SITTAH.

His source of opulence is more productive And more exhaustless than a cave of Mammon.

SALADIN.

He trades, I hear.

SITTAH.

His ships fill every harbour; His caravans through every desert toil. This has Al-Hafi told me long ago: With transport adding then--how nobly Nathan Bestows what he esteems it not a meanness By prudent industry to have justly earned - How free from prejudice his lofty soul - His heart to every virtue how unlocked - With every lovely feeling how familiar.

SALADIN.

Yet Hafi spake just now so coldly of him.

SITTAH.

Not coldly; but with awkwardness, confusion, As if he thought it dangerous to praise him, And yet knew not to blame him undeserving, Or can it really be that e'en the best Among a people cannot quite escape The tinges of the tribe; and that, in fact, Al-Hafi has in this to blush for Nathan? Be that as't may--be he the Jew or no - Is he but rich--that is enough for us.

SALADIN.

You would not, sister, take his wealth by force.

SITTAH.

What do you mean by force--fire, sword? Oh no! What force is necessary with the weak But their own weakness? Come awhile with me Into my harem: I have bought a songstress, You have not heard her, she came yesterday: Meanwhile I'll think somewhat about a project I have upon this Nathan. Follow, brother.

SCENE--The Place of Palms, close to Nathan's House.

NATHAN, attired, comes out with RECHA.
RECHA.
You have been so very slow, my dearest father, You now will hardly be in time to find him.
NATHAN.
Well, if not here beneath the palms; yet, surely, Elsewhere. My child, be satisfied. See, see, Is not that Daya making towards us?
RECHA.
She certainly has lost him then.
NATHAN.
   Why so?
RECHA.
Else she'd walk quicker.
NATHAN.
   She may not have seen us.
RECHA.
There, now she sees us.
NATHAN.
   And her speed redoubles, Be calm, my Recha.
RECHA.
   Would you have your daughter Be cool and unconcerned who 'twas that saved her, Heed not to whom is due the life she prizes Chiefly because she owed it first to thee?
NATHAN.
I would not wish thee other than thou art, E'en if I knew that in thy secret soul A very different emotion throbs.

RECHA.

Why--what my father?

NATHAN.

Dost thou ask of me, So tremblingly of me, what passes in thee? Whatever 'tis, 'tis innocence and nature. Be not alarmed, it gives me no alarm; But promise me that, when thy heart shall speak A plainer language, thou wilt not conceal A single of thy wishes from my fondness.

RECHA.

Oh the mere possibility of wishing Rather to veil and hide them makes me shudder.

NATHAN.

Let this be spoken once for all. Well, Daya -

NATHAN, RECHA, and DAYA.

DAYA.

He still is here beneath the palms, and soon Will reach yon wall. See, there he comes.

RECHA.

And seems Irresolute where next; if left or right.

DAYA.

I know he mostly passes to the convent, And therefore comes this path. What will you lay me?

RECHA.

Oh yes he does. And did you speak to him? How did he seem to-day?

DAYA.

As heretofore.

NATHAN.

Don't let him see you with me: further back; Or rather to the house.

RECHA.

Just one peep more. Now the hedge steals him from me.

DAYA.

Come away. Your father's in the right--should he perceive us, 'Tis very probable he'll tack about.

RECHA.

But for the hedge -
NATHAN.

   Now he emerges from it. He can't but see you: hence--I ask it of you.
DAYA.

I know a window whence we yet may -
RECHA.

   Ay.
[Goes in with Daya.
NATHAN.

I'm almost shy of this strange fellow, almost Shrink back from his rough virtue. That one man Should ever make another man feel awkward! And yet--He's
coming--ha!--by God, the youth Looks like a man. I love his daring eye, His open
gait. May be the shell is bitter; But not the kernel surely. I have seen Some such,
methinks. Forgive me, noble Frank.
   NATHAN and TEMPLAR.
   TEMPLAR.
What?
NATHAN.

   Give me leave.
TEMPLAR.

   Well, Jew, what wouldst thou have?
NATHAN.

The liberty of speaking to you!
TEMPLAR.

   So - Can I prevent it? Quick then, what's your business?
NATHAN.

Patience--nor hasten quite so proudly by A man, who has not merited con-
tempt, And whom, for evermore, you've made your debtor.
   TEMPLAR.

How so? Perhaps I guess--No--Are you then -
NATHAN.

My name is Nathan, father to the maid Your generous courage snatched from
circling flames, And hasten -

TEMPLAR.

If with thanks, keep, keep them all. Those little things I've had to suffer much from: Too much already, far. And, after all, You owe me nothing. Was I ever told She was your daughter? 'Tis a templar's duty To rush to the assistance of the first Poor wight that needs him; and my life just then Was quite a burden. I was mighty glad To risk it for another; tho' it were That of a Jewess.

NATHAN.

Noble, and yet shocking! The turn might be expected. Modest greatness Wears willingly the mask of what is shocking To scare off admiration: but, altho' She may disdain the tribute, admiration, Is there no other tribute she can bear with? Knight, were you here not foreign, not a captive I would not ask so freely. Speak, command, In what can I be useful?

TEMPLAR.

You--in nothing.

NATHAN.

I'm rich.

TEMPLAR.

To me the richer Jew ne'er seemed The bettor Jew.

NATHAN.

Is that a reason why You should not use the better part of him, His wealth?

TEMPLAR.

Well, well, I'll not refuse it wholly, For my poor mantle's sake--when that is threadbare, And spite of darning will not hold together, I'll come and borrow cloth, or money of thee, To make me up a new one. Don't look solemn; The danger is not pressing; 'tis not yet At the last gasp, but tight and strong and good, Save this poor corner, where an ugly spot You see is singed upon it. It got singed As I bore off your daughter from the fire.

NATHAN (taking hold of the mantle).

'Tis singular that such an ugly spot Bears better testimony to the man Than his own mouth. This brand--Oh I could kiss it! Your pardon--that I meant not.

TEMPLAR.

What?

NATHAN.

A tear Fell on the spot.

TEMPLAR.

You'll find up more such tears - (This Jew methinks begins to work upon me).

NATHAN.

Would you send once this mantle to my daughter?

TEMPLAR.

Why?

NATHAN.

That her lips may cling to this dear speck; For at her benefactor's feet to fall, I find, she hopes in vain.

TEMPLAR.

But, Jew, your name You said was Nathan--Nathan, you can join Your words together cunningly--right well - I am confused--in fact--I would have been -

NATHAN.

Twist, writhe, disguise you, as you will, I know you, You were too honest, knight, to be more civil; A girl all feeling, and a she-attendant All complaisance, a father at a distance - You valued her good name, and would not see her. You scorned to try her, lest you should be victor; For that I also thank you.

TEMPLAR.

I confess, You know how templars ought to think.

NATHAN.

Still templars - And only OUGHT to think--and all because The rules and vows enjoin it to the ORDER - I know how good men think--know that all lands Produce good men.

TEMPLAR.

But not without distinction.

NATHAN.

In colour, dress, and shape, perhaps, distinguished.

TEMPLAR.

Here more, there fewer sure?

NATHAN.

That boots not much, The great man everywhere has need of room. Too many set together only serve To crush each others' branches. Middling good, As we are, spring up everywhere in plenty. Only let one not scar and bruise the other; Let not the gnarl be angry with the stump; Let not the upper branch alone pretend Not to have started from the common earth.

TEMPLAR.

Well said: and yet, I trust, you know the nation, That first began to strike at fellow men, That first baptised itself the chosen people - How now if I were--not to hate this people, Yet for its pride could not forbear to scorn it, The pride which it to Mussulman and Christian Bequeathed, as were its God alone the true one, You start, that I, a Christian and a templar, Talk thus. Where, when, has e'er the pious rage To own the better god--on the whole world To force this better, as the best of all - Shown itself more, and in a blacker form, Than here, than now? To him, whom, here and now, The film is not removing from his eye - But be he blind that wills! Forget my speeches And leave me.

NATHAN.

Ah! indeed you do not know How closer I shall cling to you henceforth. We must, we will be friends. Despise my nation - We did not choose a nation for ourselves. Are we our nations? What's a nation then? Were Jews and Christians such, e'er they were men? And have I found in thee one more, to whom It is enough to be a man?

TEMPLAR.

That hast thou. Nathan, by God, thou hast. Thy hand. I blush To have mistaken thee a single instant.

NATHAN.

And I am proud of it. Only common souls We seldom err in.

TEMPLAR.

And uncommon ones Seldom forget. Yes, Nathan, yes we must, We will be friends.

NATHAN.

We are so. And my Recha - She will rejoice. How sweet the wider prospect That dawns upon me! Do but know her--once.

TEMPLAR.

I am impatient for it. Who is that Bursts from your house, methinks it is your

Daya.

NATHAN.

Ay--but so anxiously -

TEMPLAR.

　Sure, to our Recha Nothing has happened.

NATHAN, TEMPLAR, and DAYA.

DAYA.

　Nathan, Nathan.

NATHAN.

　Well.

DAYA.

Forgive me, knight, that I must interrupt you.

NATHAN.

What is the matter?

TEMPLAR.

　What?

DAYA.

　The sultan sends - The sultan wants to see you--in a hurry. Jesus! the sultan

-

NATHAN.

　Saladin wants me? He will be curious to see what wares, Precious, or new, I brought with me from Persia. Say there is nothing hardly yet unpacked.

DAYA.

No, no: 'tis not to look at anything. He wants to speak to you, to you in person, And orders you to come as soon as may be.

NATHAN.

I'll go--return.

DAYA.

　Knight, take it not amiss; But we were so alarmed for what the sultan Could have in view.

NATHAN.

　That I shall soon discover.

NATHAN and TEMPLAR.

TEMPLAR.

And don't you know him yet, I mean his person?

NATHAN.

Whose, Saladin's? Not yet. I've neither shunned, Nor sought to see him. And the general voice Speaks too well of him, for me not to wish, Rather to take its language upon trust, Than sift the truth out. Yet--if it be so - He, by the saving of your life, has now -

TEMPLAR.

Yes: it is so. The life I live he gave.

NATHAN.

And in it double treble life to me. This flings a bond about me, which shall tie me For ever to his service: and I scarcely Like to defer inquiring for his wishes. For everything I am ready; and am ready To own that 'tis on your account I am so.

TEMPLAR.

As often as I've thrown me in his way, I have not found as yet the means to thank him. The impression that I made upon him came Quickly, and so has vanished. Now perhaps He recollects me not, who knows? Once more At least, he must recall me to his mind, Fully to fix my doom. 'Tis not enough That by his order I am yet in being, By his permission live, I have to learn According to whose will I must exist.

NATHAN.

Therefore I shall the more avoid delay. Perchance some word may furnish me occasion To glance at you--perchance--Excuse me, knight, I am in haste. When shall we see you with us?

TEMPLAR.

Soon as I may.

NATHAN.

    That is, whene'er you will.

TEMPLAR.

To-day, then.

NATHAN.

    And your name?

TEMPLAR.

My name was--is Conrade of Stauffen.

NATHAN.

Conrade of Stauffen! Stauffen!

TEMPLAR.

Why does that strike so forcibly upon you?

NATHAN.

There are more races of that name, no doubt.

TEMPLAR.

Yes, many of that name were here--rot here. My uncle even--I should say, my father. But wherefore is your look so sharpened on me?

NATHAN.

Nothing--how can I weary to behold you -

TEMPLAR.

Therefore I quit you first. The searching eye Finds often more than it desires to see. I fear it, Nathan. Fare thee well. Let time, Not curiosity make us acquainted.

[Goes.

NATHAN, and soon after, DAYA.

NATHAN.

"The searching eye will oft discover more Than it desires," 'tis as he read my soul. That too may chance to me. 'Tis not alone Leonard's walk, stature, but his very voice. Leonard so wore his head, was even wont Just so to brush his eyebrows with his hand, As if to mask the fire that fills his look. Those deeply graven images at times How they will slumber in us, seem forgotten, When all at once a word a tone, a gesture, Retraces all. Of Stauffen? Ay right--right - Filnek and Stauffen--I will soon know more - But first to Saladin--Ha, Daya there? Why on the watch? Come nearer. By this time, I'll answer for't, you've something more at heart Than to know what the sultan wants with me.

DAYA.

And do you take it ill in part of her? You were beginning to converse with him More confidentially, just as the message, Sent by the sultan, tore us from the window.

NATHAN.

Go tell her that she may expect his visit At every instant.

DAYA.

What indeed--indeed?

NATHAN.

I think I can rely upon thee, Daya: Be on thy guard, I beg. Thou'lt not repent it. Be but discreet. Thy conscience too will surely Find its account in 't. Do not mar my plans But leave them to themselves. Relate and question With modesty, with backwardness.

DAYA.

Oh fear not. How come you to preach up all this to me? I go--go too. The sultan sends for you A second time, and by your friend Al-Hafi.

NATHAN and HAFI.

HAFI.

Ha! art thou here? I was now seeking for thee.

NATHAN.

Why in such haste? What wants he then with me?

HAFI.

Who?

NATHAN.

Saladin. I'm coming--I am coming.

HAFI.

Where, to the sultan's?

NATHAN.

Was 't not he who sent thee?

HAFI.

Me? No. And has he sent already?

NATHAN.

Yes.

HAFI.

Then 'tis all right.

NATHAN.

What's right?

HAFI.

That I'm unguilty. God knows I am not guilty, knows I said - What said I not of thee--belied thee--slandered - To ward it off.

NATHAN.

   To ward off what--be plain.

HAFI.

That them art now become his defterdar. I pity thee. Behold it I will not. I go this very hour--my road I told thee. Now--hast thou orders by the way--command, And then, adieu. Indeed they must not be Such business as a naked man can't carry. Quick, what's thy pleasure?

NATHAN.

      Recollect yourself. As yet all this is quite a riddle to me. I know of nothing.

HAFI.

   Where are then thy bags?

NATHAN.

Bags?

HAFI.

   Bags of money: bring the weightiest forth: The money thou'rt to lend the sultan, Nathan.

NATHAN.

And is that all?

HAFI.

   Novice, thou'st yet to learn How he day after day will scoop and scoop, Till nothing but an hollow empty paring, A husk as light as film, is left behind. Thou'st yet to learn how prodigality From prudent bounty's never-empty coffers Borrows and borrows, till there's not a purse Left to keep rats from starving. Thou mayst fancy That he who wants thy gold will heed thy counsel; But when has he yet listened to advice? Imagine now what just befell me with him.

NATHAN.

Well -

HAFI.

   I went in and found him with his sister, Engaged, or rather rising up from chess. Sittah plays--not amiss. Upon the board The game, that Saladin supposed was lost And had given up, yet stood. When I drew nigh, And had examined it, I soon discovered It was not gone by any means.

NATHAN.

　For you A blest discovery, a treasure-trove.

HAFI.

He only needed to remove his king Behind the tower t' have got him out of check. Could I but make you sensible -

NATHAN.

　I'll trust thee.

HAFI.

Then with the knight still left.--I would have shown him And called him to the board.--He must have won; But what d'ye think he did?

NATHAN.

　Dared doubt your insight?

HAFI.

He would not listen; but with scorn o'erthrew The standing pieces.

NATHAN.

　Is that possible?

HAFI.

And said, he chose to be check-mate--he chose it - Is that to play the game?

NATHAN.

　Most surely not: 'Tis to play with the game.

HAFI.

　And yet the stake Was not a nut-shell.

NATHAN.

　Money here or there Matters but little. Not to listen to thee, And on a point of such importance, Hafi, There lies the rub. Not even to admire Thine eagle eye--thy comprehensive glance - That calls for vengeance: --does it not, Al-Hafi?

HAFI.

I only tell it to thee that thou mayst see How his brain's formed. I bear with him no longer. Here I've been running to each dirty Moor, Inquiring who will lend him. I, who ne'er Went for myself a begging, go a borrowing, And that for others. Borrowing's much the same As begging; just as lending upon usury Is much the same as thieving--decency Makes not of lewdness virtue. On the Ganges, Among my ghebers, I have need of neither: Nor need I be the tool or pimp of either - Upon the Ganges only there are men. Here, thou alone art somehow almost worthy To have lived upon the Ganges. Wilt thou with me? And leave him with the captive cloak alone, The booty that he wants to strip thee of. Little by little he will flay thee clean. Thins thou'lt be quit at once, without the tease Of being sliced to death. Come wilt thou with me? I'll find thee with a staff.

NATHAN.

I should have thought, Come what come may, that thy resource remained: But I'll consider of it. Stay.

HAFI.

Consider - No; such things must not be considered.

NATHAN.

Stay: Till I have seen the sultan--till you've had -

HAFI.

He, who considers, looks about for motives To forbear daring. He, who can't resolve In storm and sunshine to himself to live, Must live the slave of others all his life. But as you please; farewell! 'tis you who choose. My path lies yonder--and yours there -

NATHAN.

Al-Hafi, Stay then; at least you'll set things right--not leave them At sixes and at sevens -

HAFI.

Farce! Parade! The balance in the chest will need no telling. And my account--Sittah, or you, will vouch. Farewell.

[Goes.

NATHAN.

Yes I will vouch it. Honest, wild - How shall I call you--Ah! the real beggar Is, after all, the only real monarch.

ACT III.

SCENE--A Room in Nathan's House.

RECHA and DAYA.
RECHA.

What, Daya, did my father really say I might expect him, every instant, here? That meant--now did it not? he would come soon. And yet how many instants have rolled by! - But who would think of those that are elapsed? - To the next moment only I'm alive. - At last the very one will come that brings him.

DAYA.

But for the sultan's ill-timed message, Nathan Had brought him in.

RECHA.

   And when this moment comes, And when this warmest inmost of my wishes Shall be fulfilled, what then? what then?

DAYA.

   What then? Why then I hope the warmest of my wishes Will have its turn, and happen.

RECHA.

   'Stead of this, What wish shall take possession of my bosom, Which now without some ruling wish of wishes Knows not to heave? Shall nothing? ah, I shudder.

DAYA.

Yes: mine shall then supplant the one fulfilled - My wish to see thee placed one day in Europe In hands well worthy of thee.

RECHA.

   No, thou errest - The very thing that makes thee form this wish Prevents its being mine. The country draws thee, And shall not mine retain me? Shall an image, A fond remembrance of thy home, thy kindred, Which years and distance have not yet effaced, Be mightier o'er thy soul, than what I hear, See, feel, and hold, of mine.

DAYA.

'Tis vain to struggle - The ways of heaven are the ways of heaven. Is he the destined saviour, by whose arm His God, for whom he fights, intends to lead thee Into the land, which thou wast born for -

RECHA.

Daya, What art thou prating of? My dearest Daya, Indeed thou hast some strange unseemly notions. "HIS God--FOR whom he fights"--what is a God Belonging to a man--needing another To fight his battles? And can we pronounce FOR which among the scattered clods of earth You, I was born; unless it be for that ON which we were produced. If Nathan heard thee - What has my father done to thee, that thou Hast ever sought to paint my happiness As lying far remote from him and his. What has he done to thee that thus, among The seeds of reason, which he sowed unmixed, Pure in my soul, thou ever must be seeking To plant the weeds, or flowers, of thy own land. He wills not of these pranking gaudy blossoms Upon this soil. And I too must acknowledge I feel as if they had a sour-sweet odour, That makes me giddy--that half suffocates. Thy head is wont to bear it. I don't blame Those stronger nerves that can support it. Mine - Mine it behoves not. Latterly thy angel Had made me half a fool. I am ashamed, Whene'er I see my father, of the folly.

DAYA.

As if here only wisdom were at home - Folly--if I dared speak.

RECHA.

And dar'st thou not? When was I not all ear, if thou beganst To talk about the heroes of thy faith? Have I not freely on their deeds bestowed My admiration, to their sufferings yielded The tribute of my tears? Their faith indeed Has never seemed their most heroic side To me: yet, therefore, have I only learnt To find more consolation in the thought, That our devotion to the God of all Depends not on our notions about God. My father has so often told us so - Thou hast so often to this point consented - How can it be that thou alone art restless To undermine what you built up together? This is not the most fit discussion, Daya, To usher in our friend to; tho' indeed I should not disincline to it--for to me It is of infinite importance if He too--but hark--there's some one at the door. If it were he--stay--hush -

(A Slave who shows in the Templar.)

They are--here this way.

TEMPLAR, DAYA, and RECHA.

RECHA.

(starts--composes herself--then offers to fall at his feet) 'Tis he--my saviour! ah!

TEMPLAR.

This to avoid Have I alone deferred my call so long.

RECHA.

Yes, at the feet of this proud man, I will Thank--God alone. The man will have no thanks; No more than will the bucket which was busy In showering watery damps upon the flame. That was filled, emptied--but to me, to thee What boots it? So the man--he too, he too Was thrust, he knew not how, and the fire. I dropped, by chance, into his open arm. By chance, remained there--like a fluttering spark Upon his mantle--till--I know not what Pushed us both from amid the conflagration. What room is here for thanks? How oft in Europe Wine urges men to very different deeds! Templars must so behave; it is their office, Like better taught or rather handier spaniels, To fetch from out of fire, as out of water.

TEMPLAR.

Oh Daya, Daya, if, in hasty moments Of care and of chagrin, my unchecked temper Betrayed me into rudeness, why convey To her each idle word that left my tongue? This is too piercing a revenge indeed; Yet if henceforth thou wilt interpret better -

DAYA.

I question if these barbed words, Sir Knight, Alighted so, as to have much disserved you.

RECHA.

How, you had cares, and were more covetous Of them than of your life?

TEMPLAR.

[who has been viewing her with wonder and perturbation].

Thou best of beings, How is my soul 'twixt eye and ear divided! No: 'twas not she I snatched from amid fire: For who could know her and forbear to do it? - Indeed--disguised by terror - [Pause: during which he gazes on her as it were entranced.

RECHA.

But to me You still appear the same you then appeared.

[Another like pause--till she resumes, in order to interrupt him.

Now tell me, knight, where have you been so long? It seems as might I ask-- where are you now?

TEMPLAR.

I am--where I perhaps ought not to be.

RECHA.

Where have you been? where you perhaps ought not - That is not well.

TEMPLAR.

Up--how d'ye call the mountain? Up Sinai.

RECHA.

Oh, that's very fortunate. Now I shall learn for certain if 'tis true -

TEMPLAR.

What! if the spot may yet be seen where Moses Stood before God; when first -

RECHA.

No, no, not that. Where'er he stood, 'twas before God. Of this I know enough already. Is it true, I wish to learn from you that--that it is not By far so troublesome to climb this mountain As to get down--for on all mountains else, That I have seen, quite the reverse obtains. Well, knight, why will you turn away from me? Not look at me?

TEMPLAR.

Because I wish to hear you.

RECHA.

Because you do not wish me to perceive You smile at my simplicity--You smile That I can think of nothing more important To ask about the holy hill of hills: Do you not?

TEMPLAR.

Must I meet those eyes again? And now you cast them down, and damp the

smile - Am I in doubtful motions of the features To read what I so plainly hear--
what you So audibly declare; yet will conceal? - How truly said thy father "Do but
know her!"

RECHA.

Who has--of whom--said so to thee?

TEMPLAR.

   Thy father Said to me "Do but know her," and of thee.

DAYA.

And have not I too said so, times and oft.

TEMPLAR.

But where is then your father--with the sultan?

RECHA.

So I suppose.

TEMPLAR.

   Yet there? Oh, I forget, He cannot be there still. He is waiting for me Most
certainly below there by the cloister. 'Twas so, I think, we had agreed, Forgive, I go
in quest of him.

DAYA.

   Knight, I'll do that. Wait here, I'll bring him hither instantly.

TEMPLAR.

Oh no--Oh no. He is expecting me. Besides--you are not aware what may have
happened. 'Tis not unlikely he may be involved With Saladin--you do not know the
sultan - In some unpleasant--I must go, there's danger If I forbear.

RECHA.

   Danger--of what? of what?

TEMPLAR.

Danger for me, for thee, for him; unless I go at once. [Goes.

RECHA and DAYA.

RECHA.

   What is the matter, Daya? So quick--what comes across him, drives him
hence?

DAYA.

Let him alone, I think it no bad sign.

RECHA.

Sign--and of what?

DAYA.

That something passes in him. It boils--but it must not boil over. Leave
him - Now 'tis your turn.

RECHA.

My turn? Thou dost become Like him incomprehensible to me.

DAYA.

Now you may give him back all that unrest He once occasioned. Be not too
severe, Nor too vindictive.

RECHA.

Daya, what you mean You must know best.

DAYA.

And pray are you again So calm.

RECHA.

I am--yes that I am.

DAYA.

At least Own--that this restlessness has given you pleasure, And that you
have to thank his want of ease For what of ease you now enjoy.

RECHA.

Of that I am unconscious. All I could confess Were, that it does seem
strange unto myself, How, in this bosom, such a pleasing calm Can suddenly suc-
ceed to such a tossing.

DAYA.

His countenance, his speech, his manner, has By this the satiated thee.

RECHA.

Satiated, I will not say--not by a good deal yet.

DAYA.

But satisfied the more impatient craving.

RECHA.

Well, well, if you must have it so.

DAYA.

I? no.

RECHA.

To me he will be ever dear, will ever Remain more dear than my own life; altho' My pulse no longer flutters at his name, My heart no longer, when I think about him, Beats stronger, swifter. What have I been prating? Come, Daya, let us once more to the window Which overlooks the palms.

DAYA.

So that 'tis not Yet satisfied--the more impatient craving.

RECHA.

Now I shall see the palm-trees once again, Not him alone amid them.

DAYA.

This cold fit Is but the harbinger of other fevers.

RECHA.

Cold--cold--I am not cold; but I observe not Less willingly what I behold with calmness.

SCENE--An Audience Room in the Sultan's Palace.

SITTAH: SALADIN giving directions at the door.

SALADIN.

Here, introduce the Jew, whene'er he comes - He seems in no great haste.

SITTAH.

May be at first He was not in the way.

SALADIN.

Ah, sister, sister!

SITTAH.

You seem as if a combat were impending.

SALADIN.

With weapons that I have not learnt to wield. Must I disguise myself? I use precautions? I lay a snare? When, where gained I that knowledge? And this, for what? To fish for money--money - For money from a Jew--and to such arts Must Saladin descend at last to come at The least of little things?

SITTAH.

Each little thing Despised too much finds methods of revenge.

SALADIN.

'Tis but too true. And if this Jew should prove The fair good man, as once the dervis painted -

SITTAH.

Then difficulties cease. A snare concerns The avaricious, cautious, fearful Jew; And not the good wise man: for he is ours Without a snare. Then the delight of hearing How such a man speaks out; with what stern strength He tears the net, or with what prudent foresight He one by one undoes the tangled meshes; That will be all to boot -

SALADIN.

That I shall joy in.

SITTAH.

What then should trouble thee? For if he be One of the many only, a mere Jew, You will not blush to such a one to seem A man, as he thinks all mankind to be. One, that to him should bear a better aspect, Would seem a fool--a dupe.

SALADIN.

So that I must Act badly, lest the bad think badly of me.

SITTAH.

Yes, if you call it acting badly, brother, To use a thing after its kind.

SALADIN.

There's nothing That woman's wit invents it can't embellish.

SITTAH.

Embellish -

SALADIN.

But their fine-wrought filligree In my rude hand would break. It is for those That can contrive them to employ such weapons: They ask a practised wrist. But chance what may, Well as I can -

SITTAH.

Trust not yourself too little. I answer for you, if you have the will. Such men as you would willingly persuade us It was their swords, their swords alone that raised them. The lion's apt to be ashamed of hunting In fellowship of the fox--'tis of his fellow Not of the cunning that he is ashamed.

SALADIN.

You women would so gladly level man Down to yourselves. Go, I have got my lesson.

SITTAH.

What--MUST I go?

SALADIN.

   Had you the thought of staying?

SITTAH.

In your immediate presence not indeed, But in the by-room.

SALADIN.

   You could like to listen. Not that, my sister, if I may insist. Away! the curtain rustles--he is come. Beware of staying--I'll be on the watch.

[While Sittah retires through one door, Nathan enters at another, and Saladin seats himself.]

SALADIN and NATHAN.

SALADIN.

Draw nearer, Jew, yet nearer; here, quite by me, Without all fear.

NATHAN.

   Remain that for thy foes!

SALADIN.

Your name is Nathan?

NATHAN.

   Yes.

SALADIN.

   Nathan the wise?

NATHAN.

No.

SALADIN.

   If not thou, the people calls thee so.

NATHAN.

May be, the people.

SALADIN.

   Fancy not that I Think of the people's voice contemptuously; I have been wishing much to know the man Whom it has named the wise.

NATHAN.

And if it named Him so in scorn. If wise meant only prudent. And prudent, one who knows his interest well.

SALADIN.

Who knows his real interest, thou must mean.

NATHAN.

Then were the interested the most prudent, Then wise and prudent were the same.

SALADIN.

I hear You proving what your speeches contradict. You know man's real interests, which the people Knows not--at least have studied how to know them. That alone makes the sage.

NATHAN.

Which each imagines Himself to be.

SALADIN.

Of modesty enough! Ever to meet it, where one seeks to hear Dry truth, is vexing. Let us to the purpose - But, Jew, sincere and open -

NATHAN.

I will serve thee So as to merit, prince, thy further notice.

SALADIN.

Serve me--how?

NATHAN.

Thou shalt have the best I bring. Shalt have them cheap.

SALADIN.

What speak you of?--your wares? My sister shall be called to bargain with you For them (so much for the sly listener), I Have nothing to transact now with the merchant.

NATHAN.

Doubtless then you would learn, what, on my journey, I noticed of the motions of the foe, Who stirs anew. If unreserved I may -

SALADIN.

Neither was that the object of my sending: I know what I have need to know already. In short I willed your presence -

NATHAN.

    Sultan, order.

SALADIN.

To gain instruction quite on other points. Since you are a man so wise, tell me which law, Which faith appears to you the better?

NATHAN.

    Sultan, I am a Jew.

SALADIN.

    And I a Mussulman: The Christian stands between us. Of these three Religions only one came be the true. A man, like you, remains not just where birth Has chanced to cast him, or, if he remains there, Does it from insight, choice, from grounds of preference. Share then with me your insight--let me hear The grounds of preference, which I have wanted The leisure to examine--learn the choice, These grounds have motived, that it may be mine. In confidence I ask it. How you startle, And weigh me with your eye! It may well be I'm the first sultan to whom this caprice, Methinks not quite unworthy of a sultan, Has yet occurred. Am I not? Speak then--Speak. Or do you, to collect yourself, desire Some moments of delay--I give them you - (Whether she's listening?--I must know of her If I've done right.) Reflect--I'll soon return -

[Saladin steps into the room to which Sittah had retired.]

NATHAN.

Strange! how is this? what wills the sultan of me? I came prepared with cash-- he asks truth. Truth? As if truth too were cash--a coin disused That goes by weight- -indeed 'tis some such thing - But a new coin, known by the stamp at once, To be flung down and told upon the counter, It is not that. Like gold in bags tied up, So truth lies hoarded in the wise man's head To be brought out.--Which now in this transaction Which of us plays the Jew; he asks for truth, Is truth what he requires, his aim, his end? That this is but the glue to lime a snare Ought not to be suspected, 'twere too little, Yet what is found too little for the great - In fact, through hedge and pale to stalk at once Into one's field beseems not--friends look round, Seek for the path, ask leave to pass the gate - I must be cautious. Yet to damp him back, And be the stubborn Jew is not the thing; And wholly to throw off the Jew, still less. For if no Jew he might with right inquire - Why not a Mussulman--Yes--that may serve me. Not children only can be quieted With stories. Ha! he comes--well, let him come.

SALADIN (returning).

So, there, the field is clear, I'm not too quick, Thou hast bethought thyself as much as need is, Speak, no one hears.

NATHAN.

  Might the whole world but hear us.

SALADIN.

Is Nathan of his cause so confident? Yes, that I call the sage--to veil no truth, For truth to hazard all things, life and goods.

NATHAN.

Aye, when 'tis necessary and when useful.

SALADIN.

Henceforth I hope I shall with reason bear One of my titles--"Betterer of the world And of the law."

NATHAN.

  In truth a noble title. But, sultan, e'er I quite unfold myself Allow me to relate a tale.

SALADIN.

  Why not? I always was a friend of tales well told.

NATHAN.

Well told, that's not precisely my affair.

SALADIN.

Again so proudly modest, come begin.

NATHAN.

In days of yore, there dwelt in east a man Who from a valued hand received a ring Of endless worth: the stone of it an opal, That shot an ever-changing tint: moreover, It had the hidden virtue him to render Of God and man beloved, who in this view, And this persuasion, wore it. Was it strange The eastern man ne'er drew it off his finger, And studiously provided to secure it For ever to his house. Thus-- He bequeathed it; First, to the MOST BELOVED of his sons, Ordained that he again should leave the ring To the MOST DEAR among his children--and That without heeding birth, the FAVOURITE son, In virtue of the ring alone, should always Remain the lord o' th' house--You hear me, Sultan?

SALADIN.

I understand thee--on.

NATHAN.

From son to son, At length this ring descended to a father, Who had three sons, alike obedient to him; Whom therefore he could not but love alike. At times seemed this, now that, at times the third, (Accordingly as each apart received The overflowings of his heart) most worthy To heir the ring, which with good-natured weakness He privately to each in turn had promised. This went on for a while. But death approached, And the good father grew embarrassed. So To disappoint two sons, who trust his promise, He could not bear. What's to be done. He sends In secret to a jeweller, of whom, Upon the model of the real ring, He might bespeak two others, and commanded To spare nor cost nor pains to make them like, Quite like the true one. This the artist managed. The rings were brought, and e'en the father's eye Could not distinguish which had been the model. Quite overjoyed he summons all his sons, Takes leave of each apart, on each bestows His blessing and his ring, and dies--Thou hearest me?

SALADIN.

I hear, I hear, come finish with thy tale; Is it soon ended?

NATHAN.

It is ended, Sultan, For all that follows may be guessed of course. Scarce is the father dead, each with his ring Appears, and claims to be the lord o' th' house. Comes question, strife, complaint--all to no end; For the true ring could no more be distinguished Than now can--the true faith.

SALADIN.

How, how, is that To be the answer to my query?

NATHAN.

No, But it may serve as my apology; If I can't venture to decide between Rings, which the father got expressly made, That they might not be known from one another.

SALADIN.

The rings--don't trifle with me; I must think That the religions which I named can be Distinguished, e'en to raiment, drink and food,

NATHAN.

And only not as to their grounds of proof. Are not all built alike on history, Traditional, or written. History Must be received on trust--is it not so? In whom now are we likeliest to put trust? In our own people surely, in those men Whose blood we are, in them, who from our childhood Have given us proofs of love, who ne'er deceived us, Unless 'twere wholesomer to be deceived. How can I less believe in my forefathers Than thou in thine. How can I ask of thee To own that thy forefathers falsified In order to yield mine the praise of truth. The like of Christians.

SALADIN.

By the living God, The man is in the right, I must be silent.

NATHAN.

Now let us to our rings return once more. As said, the sons complained. Each to the judge Swore from his father's hand immediately To have received the ring, as was the case; After he had long obtained the father's promise, One day to have the ring, as also was. The father, each asserted, could to him Not have been false, rather than so suspect Of such a father, willing as he might be With charity to judge his brethren, he Of treacherous forgery was bold t' accuse them.

SALADIN.

Well, and the judge, I'm eager now to hear What thou wilt make him say. Go on, go on.

NATHAN.

The judge said, If ye summon not the father Before my seat, I cannot give a sentence. Am I to guess enigmas? Or expect ye That the true ring should here unseal its lips? But hold--you tell me that the real ring Enjoys the hidden power to make the wearer Of God and man beloved; let that decide. Which of you do two brothers love the best? You're silent. Do these love-exciting rings Act inward only, not without? Does each Love but himself? Ye're all deceived deceivers, None of your rings is true. The real ring Perhaps is gone. To hide or to supply Its loss, your father ordered three for one.

SALADIN.

O charming, charming!

NATHAN.

And (the judge continued) If you will take advice in lieu of sentence, This is my counsel to you, to take up The matter where it stands. If each of you Has had a ring presented by his father, Let each believe his own the real ring. 'Tis possible the father chose no longer To tolerate the one ring's tyranny; And certainly, as he much loved you all, And loved you all alike, it could not please him By favouring one to be of two the oppressor. Let each feel honoured by this free affection. Un-warped of prejudice; let each endeavour To vie with both his brothers in displaying The virtue of his ring; assist its might With gentleness, benevolence, forbearance, With inward resignation to the godhead, And if the virtues of the ring continue To show themselves among your children's children, After a thousand thousand years, appear Before this judgment-seat--a greater one Than I shall sit upon it, and decide. So spake the modest judge.

SALADIN.

   God!

NATHAN.

   Saladin, Feel'st thou thyself this wiser, promised man?

SALADIN.

I dust, I nothing, God!

[Precipitates himself upon Nathan, and takes hold of his hand, which he does not quit the remainder of the scene.]

NATHAN.

   What moves thee, Sultan?

SALADIN.

Nathan, my dearest Nathan, 'tis not yet The judge's thousand thousand years are past, His judgment-seat's not mine. Go, go, but love me.

NATHAN.

Has Saladin then nothing else to order?

SALADIN.

No.

NATHAN.

   Nothing?

SALADIN.

   Nothing in the least, and wherefore?

NATHAN.

I could have wished an opportunity To lay a prayer before you.
SALADIN.

    Is there need Of opportunity for that? Speak freely.
NATHAN.

I come from a long journey from collecting Debts, and I've almost of hard cash too much; The times look perilous--I know not where To lodge it safely--I was thinking thou, For coming wars require large sums, couldst use it.
SALADIN (fixing Nathan).

Nathan, I ask not if thou sawst Al-Hafi, I'll not examine if some shrewd suspicion Spurs thee to make this offer of thyself.
NATHAN.

Suspicion -
SALADIN.

    I deserve this offer. Pardon, For what avails concealment, I acknowledge I was about -
NATHAN.

    To ask the same of me?
SALADIN.

Yes.
NATHAN.

    Then 'tis well we're both accommodated. That I can't send thee all I have of treasure Arises from the templar; thou must know him, I have a weighty debt to pay to him.
SALADIN.

A templar! How, thou dost not with thy gold Support my direst foes.
NATHAN.

    I speak of him Whose life the sultan -
SALADIN.

    What art thou recalling? I had forgot the youth, whence is he, knowest thou?
NATHAN.

Hast thou not heard then how thy clemency To him has fallen on me. He at the risk Of his new-spared existence, from the flames Rescued my daughter.

SALADIN.

Ha! Has he done that; He looked like one that would--my brother too, Whom he's so like, bad done it. Is he here still? Bring him to me--I have so often talked To Sittah of this brother, whom she knew not, That I must let her see his counterfeit. Go fetch him. How a single worthy action, Though but of whim or passion born, gives rise To other blessings! Fetch him.

NATHAN.

In an instant. The rest remains as settled.

SALADIN.

O, I wish I had let my sister listen. Well, I'll to her. How shall I make her privy to all this?

SCENE.--The Place of Palms.

[The TEMPLAR walking and agitated.]

TEMPLAR.

Here let the weary victim pant awhile. - Yet would I not have time to ascertain What passes in me; would not snuff beforehand The coming storm. 'Tis sure I fled in vain; But more than fly I could not do, whatever Comes of it. Ah! to ward it off--the blow Was given so suddenly. Long, much, I strove To keep aloof; but vainly. Once to see her - Her, whom I surely did not court the sight of, To see her, and to form the resolution, Never to lose sight of her here again, Was one--The resolution?-- Not 'tis will, Fixt purpose, made (for I was passive in it) Sealed, doomed. To see her, and to feel myself Bound to her, wove into her very being, Was one--remains one. Separate from her To live is quite unthinkable--is death. And wheresoever after death we be, There too the thought were death. And is this love? Yet so in troth the templar loves--so--so - The Christian loves the Jewess. What of that? Here in this holy land, and therefore holy And dear to me, I have already doffed Some prejudices.--Well--what says my vow? As templar I am dead, was dead to that From the same hour which made me prisoner To Saladin. But is the head he gave me My old one? No. It knows no word of what Was prated into yon, of what had bound it. It is a better; for its patrial sky Fitter than yon. I feel--I'm conscious of it, With this I now begin to think, as here My father must have thought; if tales of him Have not

been told untruly. Tales--why tales? They're credible--more credible than ever -
Now that I'm on the brink of stumbling, where He fell. He fell? I'd rather fall with
men, Than stand with children. His example pledges His approbation, and whose
approbation Have I else need of? Nathan's? Surely of his Encouragement, applause,
I've little need To doubt--O what a Jew is he! yet easy To pass for the mere Jew.
He's coming--swiftly - And looks delighted--who leaves Saladin With other looks?
Hoa, Nathan!

NATHAN and TEMPLAR.

NATHAN.

    Are you there?

TEMPLAR.

Your visit to the sultan has been long.

NATHAN.

Not very long; my going was indeed Too much delayed. Troth, Conrade, this
man's fame Outstrips him not. His fame is but his shadow. But before all I have to
tell you -

TEMPLAR.

    What?

NATHAN.

That he would speak with you, and that directly. First to my house, where I
would give some orders, Then we'll together to the sultan.

TEMPLAR.

  Nathan, I enter not thy doors again before -

NATHAN.

Then you've been there this while--have spoken with her. How do you like
my Recha?

TEMPLAR.

    Words cannot tell - Gaze on her once again--I never will - Never--no never:
unless thou wilt promise That I for ever, ever, may behold her.

NATHAN.

How should I take this?

TEMPLAR (falling suddenly upon his neck).

Nathan--O my father!

NATHAN.

Young man!

TEMPLAR (quitting him as suddenly).

Not son?--I pray thee, Nathan--ha!

NATHAN.

Thou dear young man!

TEMPLAR.

Not son?--I pray thee, Nathan, Conjure thee by the strongest bonds of nature, Prefer not those of later date, the weaker. - Be it enough to thee to be a man! Push me not from thee!

NATHAN.

Dearest, dearest friend! -

TEMPLAR.

Not son? Not son? Not even--even if Thy daughter's gratitude had in her bosom Prepared the way for love--not even if Both wait thy nod alone to be but one? - You do not speak?

NATHAN.

Young knight, you have surprised me.

TEMPLAR.

Do I surprise thee--thus surprise thee, Nathan, With thy own thought? Canst thou not in my mouth Know it again? Do I surprise you?

NATHAN.

Ere I know, which of the Stauffens was your father?

TEMPLAR.

What say you, Nathan?--And in such a moment Is curiosity your only feeling?

NATHAN.

For see, once I myself well knew a Stauffen, Whose name was Conrade.

TEMPLAR.

Well, and if my father Was bearer of that name?

NATHAN.

Indeed?

TEMPLAR.

My name Is from my father's, Conrade.

NATHAN.

Then thy father Was not my Conrade. He was, like thyself, A templar, never wedded.

TEMPLAR.

For all that -

NATHAN.

How?

TEMPLAR.

For all that he may have been my father.

NATHAN.

You joke.

TEMPLAR.

And you are captious. Boots it then To be true-born? Does bastard wound thine ear? The race is not to be despised: but hold, Spare me my pedigree; I'll spare thee thine. Not that I doubt thy genealogic tree. O, God forbid! You may attest it all As far as Abraham back; and backwarder I know it to my heart--I'll swear to it also.

NATHAN.

Knight, you grow bitter. Do I merit this? Have I refused you ought? I've but forborne To close with you at the first word--no more.

TEMPLAR.

Indeed--no more? O then forgive -

NATHAN.

'Tis well. Do but come with me.

TEMPLAR.

Whither? To thy house? No? there not--there not: 'tis a burning soil. Here I await thee, go. Am I again To see her, I shall see her times enough: If not I have already gazed too much.

NATHAN.

I'll try to be soon back. [Goes.

TEMPLAR.

Too much indeed-- Strange that the human brain, so infinite Of comprehension, yet at times will fill Quite full, and all at once, of a mere trifle - No matter what it teems with. Patience! Patience! The soul soon calms again, th' upboiling stuff Makes itself room and brings back light and order. Is this then the first time I love? Or was What by that name I knew before, not love - And this, this love alone that now I feel?

DAYA and TEMPLAR.

DAYA.

Sir knight, sir knight.

TEMPLAR.

  Who calls? ha, Daya, you?

DAYA.

I managed to slip by him. No, come here (He'll see us where you stand) behind this tree.

TEMPLAR.

Why so mysterious? What's the matter, Daya?

DAYA.

Yes, 'tis a secret that has brought me to you A twofold secret. One I only know, The other only you. Let's interchange, Intrust yours first to me, then I'll tell mine.

TEMPLAR.

With pleasure when I'm able to discover What you call me. But that yours will explain. Begin -

DAYA.

That is not fair, yours first, sir knight; For be assured my secret serves you not Unless I have yours first. If I sift it out You'll not have trusted me, and then my secret Is still my own, and yours lost all for nothing. But, knight, how can you men so fondly fancy You ever hide such secrets from us women.

TEMPLAR.

Secrets we often are unconscious of.

DAYA.

May be--So then I must at last be friendly, And break it to you. Tell me now, whence came it That all at once you started up abruptly And in the twinkling of an eye were fled? That you left us without one civil speech! That you return no more with Nathan to us - Has Recha then made such a slight impression, Or made so deep a one? I penetrate you. Think you that on a limed twig the poor bird Can flutter cheerfully, or hop at ease With its wing pinioned? Come, come, in one word Acknowledge to me plainly that you love her, Love her to madness, and I'll tell you what.

TEMPLAR.
To madness, oh, you're very penetrating.

DAYA.
Grant me the love, and I'll give up the madness.

TEMPLAR.
Because that must be understood of course - A templar love a Jewess -

DAYA.
    Seems absurd, But often there's more fitness in a thing Than we at once discern; nor were this time The first, when through an unexpected path The Saviour drew his children on to him Across the tangled maze of human life.

TEMPLAR.
So solemn that--(and yet if in the stead Of Saviour, I were to say Providence, It would sound true) you make me curious, Daya, Which I'm unwont to be.

DAYA.
    This is the place For miracles

TEMPLAR.
    For wonders--well and good - Can it be otherwise, where the whole world Presses as toward a centre. My dear Daya, Consider what you asked of me as owned; That I do love her--that I can't imagine How I should live without her--that

DAYA.
    Indeed! Then, knight, swear to me you will call her yours, Make both her present and eternal welfare.

TEMPLAR.
And how, how can I, can I swear to do What is not in my power?

DAYA.
    'Tis in your power, A single word will put it in your power.

TEMPLAR.
So that her father shall not be against it.

DAYA.

Her father--father? he shall be compelled.

TEMPLAR.

As yet he is not fallen among thieves-- Compelled?

DAYA.

Aye to be willing that you should.

TEMPLAR.

Compelled and willing--what if I inform thee That I have tried to touch this string already, It vibrates not responsive.

DAYA.

He refused thee?

TEMPLAR.

He answered in a tone of such discordance That I was hurt.

DAYA.

What do you say? How, you Betrayed the shadow of a wish for Recha, And he did not spring up for joy, drew back, Drew coldly back, made difficulties?

TEMPLAR.

Almost.

DAYA.

Well then I'll not deliberate a moment.

TEMPLAR.

And yet you are deliberating still.

DAYA.

That man was always else so good, so kind, I am so deeply in his debt. Why, why Would he not listen to you? God's my witness That my heart bleeds to come about him thus.

TEMPLAR.

I pray you, Daya, once for all, to end This dire uncertainty. But if you doubt Whether what 'tis your purpose to reveal Be right or wrong, be praiseworthy or shameful, Speak not--I will forget that you have had Something to hide.

DAYA.

That spurs me on still more. Then learn that Recha is no Jewess, that She is a Christian.

TEMPLAR.

I congratulate you, 'Twas a hard labour, but 'tis out at last; The pangs of the delivery won't hurt you. Go on with undiminished zeal, and people Heaven, when no longer fit to people earth.

DAYA.

How, knight, does my intelligence deserve Such bitter scorn? That Recha is a Christian On you a Christian templar, and her lover, Confers no joy.

TEMPLAR.

Particularly as She is a Christian of your making, Daya.

DAYA.

O, so you understand it--well and good - I wish to find out him that might convert her. It is her fate long since to have been that Which she is spoiled for being.

TEMPLAR.

Do explain - Or go.

DAYA.

She is a Christian child--of Christian Parents was born and is baptised.

TEMPLAR (hastily).

And Nathan -

DAYA.

Is not her father.

TEMPLAR.

Nathan not her father - And are you sure of what you say?

DAYA.

I am, It is a truth has cost me tears of blood. No, he is not her father.

TEMPLAR.

And has only Brought her up as his daughter, educated The Christian child a Jewess.

DAYA.

Certainly.

TEMPLAR.

And she is unacquainted with her birth? Has never learnt from him that she was born A Christian, and no Jewess?

DAYA.

Never yet.

TEMPLAR.

And he not only let the child grow up In this mistaken notion, but still leaves The woman in it.

DAYA.

Aye, alas!

TEMPLAR.

How, Nathan, The wise good Nathan thus allow himself To stifle nature's voice? Thus to misguide Upon himself th' effusions of a heart Which to itself abandoned would have formed Another bias, Daya--yes, indeed You have intrusted an important secret That may have consequences--it confounds me, I cannot tell what I've to do at present, Therefore go, give me time, he may come by And may surprise us.

DAYA.

I should drop for fright.

TEMPLAR.

I am not able now to talk, farewell; And if you chance to meet him, only say That we shall find each other at the sultan's.

DAYA.

Let him not see you've any grudge against him. That should be kept to give the proper impulse To things at last, and may remove your scruples Respecting Recha. But then, if you take her Back with you into Europe, let not me Be left behind.

TEMPLAR.

That we'll soon settle, go.

ACT IV.

SCENE.--The Cloister of a Convent. The FRIAR alone.

FRIAR.
Aye--aye--he's very right--the patriarch is - In fact of all that he has sent me after Not much turns out his way--Why put on me Such business and no other? I don't care To coax and wheedle, and to run my nose Into all sorts of things, and have a hand In all that's going forward. I did not Renounce the world, for my own part, in order To be entangled with 't for other people.
FRIAR and TEMPLAR.
TEMPLAR (abruptly entering).
Good brother, are you there? I've sought you long.
FRIAR.
Me, sir?
TEMPLAR.
   What, don't you recollect me?
FRIAR.
      Oh, I thought I never in my life was likely To see you any more. For so I hoped In God. I did not vastly relish the proposal That I was bound to make you. Yes, God knows, How little I desired to find a hearing, Knows I was inly glad when you refused Without a moment's thought, what of a knight Would be unworthy. Are your second thoughts -
TEMPLAR.
So, you already know my purpose, I Scarce know myself.
FRIAR.
   Have you by this reflected That our good patriarch is not so much out, That

gold and fame in plenty may be got By his commission, that a foe's a foe Were he our guardian angel seven times over. Have you weighed this 'gainst flesh and blood, and come To strike the bargain he proposed. Ah, God.

FRIAR.

TEMPLAR.

My dear good man, set your poor heart at ease. Not therefore am I come, not therefore wish To see the patriarch in person. Still On the first point I think as I then thought, Nor would I for aught in the world exchange That good opinion, which I once obtained From such a worthy upright man as thou art, I come to ask your patriarch's advice -

FRIAR (looking round with timidity).

Our patriarch's--you? a knight ask priest's advice?

TEMPLAR.

Mine is a priestly business.

FRIAR.

    Yet the priests Ask not the knights' advice, be their affair Ever so knightly.

TEMPLAR.

    Therefore one allows them To overshoot themselves, a privilege Which such as I don't vastly envy them. Indeed if I were acting for myself, Had not t' account with others, I should care But little for his counsel. But some things I'd rather do amiss by others' guidance Than by my own aright. And then by this time I see religion too is party, and He, who believes himself the most impartial, Does but uphold the standard of his own, Howe'er unconsciously. And since 'tis so, So must be well.

FRIAR.

    I rather shall not answer, For I don't understand exactly.

TEMPLAR.

    Yet Let me consider what it is precisely That I have need of, counsel or decision, Simple or learned counsel.--Thank you, brother, I thank you for your hint--A patriarch--why? Be thou my patriarch; for 'tis the plain Christian, Whom in the patriarch I have to consult, And not the patriarch in the Christian.

FRIAR.

    Oh, I beg no further--you must quite mistake me; He that knows much hath learnt much care, and I Devoted me to only one. 'Tis well, Most luckily here comes the very man, Wait here, stand still--he has perceived you, knight.

TEMPLAR.

I'd rather shun him, he is not my man. A thick red smiling prelate--and as stately -

FRIAR.

But you should see him on a gala-day; He only comes from visiting the sick.

TEMPLAR.

Great Saladin must then be put to shame.

[The Patriarch, after marching up one of the aisles in great pomp, draws near, and makes signs to the Friar, who approaches him.]

PATRIARCH, FRIAR, and TEMPLAR.

PATRIARCH.

Hither--was that the templar? What wants he?

FRIAR.

I know not.

PATRIARCH (approaches the templar, while the friar and the rest of his train draw back).

So, sir knight, I'm truly happy To meet the brave young man--so very young too - Something, God helping, may come of him.

TEMPLAR.

More Than is already hardly will come of him, But less, my reverend father, that may chance.

PATRIARCH.

It is my prayer at least a knight so pious May for the cause of Christendom and God Long be preserved; nor can that fail, so be Young valour will lend ear to aged counsel. With what can I be useful any way?

TEMPLAR.

With that which my youth is without, with counsel.

PATRIARCH.

Most willingly, but counsel should be followed.

TEMPLAR.

Surely not blindly?

PATRIARCH.

Who says that? Indeed None should omit to make use of the reason Given him by God, in things where it belongs, But it belongs not everywhere; for instance, If God, by some one of his blessed angels, Or other holy minister of his word, Deign'd to make known a mean, by which the welfare Of Christendom, or of his holy church, In some peculiar and especial manner Might be promoted or secured, who then Shall venture to rise up, and try by reason The will of him who has created reason, Measure th' eternal laws of heaven by The little rules of a vain human honour? - But of all this enough. What is it then On which our counsel is desired?

TEMPLAR.

Suppose, My reverend father, that a Jew possessed An only child, a girl we'll say, whom he With fond attention forms to every virtue, And loves more than his very soul; a child Who by her pious love requites his goodness. And now suppose it whispered--say to me - This girl is not the daughter of the Jew, He picked up, purchased, stole her in her childhood - That she was born of Christians and baptised, But that the Jew hath reared her as a Jewess, Allows her to remain a Jewess, and To think herself his daughter. Reverend father What then ought to be done?

PATRIARCH.

I shudder! But First will you please explain if such a case Be fact, or only an hypothesis? That is to say, if you, of your own head, Invent the case, or if indeed it happened, And still continues happening?

TEMPLAR.

I had thought That just to learn your reverence's opinion This were all one.

PATRIARCH.

All one--now see how apt Proud human reason is in spiritual things To err: 'tis not all one; for, if the point In question be a mere sport of the wit, 'Twill not be worth our while to think it through But I should recommend the curious person To theatres, where oft, with loud applause, Such pro and contras have been agitated. But if the object should be something more Than by a school-trick--by a sleight of logic To get the better of me--if the case Be really extant, if it should have happened Within our diocese, or--or perhaps Here in our dear Jerusalem itself, Why then -

TEMPLAR.

What then?

PATRIARCH.

Then were it proper To execute at once upon the Jew The penal laws in such a case provided By papal and imperial right, against So foul a crime--such dire abomination.

TEMPLAR.

So.

PATRIARCH.

And the laws forementioned have decreed, That if a Jew shall to apostacy Seduce a Christian, he shall die by fire.

TEMPLAR.

So.

PATRIARCH.

How much more the Jew, who forcibly Tears from the holy font a Christian child, And breaks the sacramental bond of baptism; For all what's done to children is by force - I mean except what the church does to children.

TEMPLAR.

What if the child, but for this fostering Jew, Must have expired in misery?

PATRIARCH.

That's nothing, The Jew has still deserved the faggot--for 'Twere better it here died in misery Than for eternal woe to live. Besides, Why should the Jew forestall the hand of God? God, if he wills to save, can save without him.

TEMPLAR.

And spite of him too save eternally.

PATRIARCH.

That's nothing! Still the Jew is to be burnt.

TEMPLAR.

That hurts me--more particularly as 'Tis said he has not so much taught the maid His faith, as brought her up with the mere knowledge Of what our reason teaches about God.

PATRIARCH.

That's nothing! Still the Jew is to be burnt - And for this very reason would deserve To be thrice burnt. How, let a child grow up Without a faith? Not even teach a child The greatest of its duties, to believe? 'Tis heinous! I am quite astonished, knight, That you yourself -

TEMPLAR.

The rest, right reverend sir, In the confessional, but not before. [Offers to go.

PATRIARCH.

What off--not stay for my interrogation - Not name to me this infidel, this Jew - Not find him up for me at once? But hold, A thought occurs, I'll straightway to the sultan Conformably to the capitulation, Which Saladin has sworn, he must support us In all the privileges, all the doctrines Which appertain to our most holy faith, Thank God, we've the original in keeping, We have his hand and seal to it--we - And I shall lead him easily to think How very dangerous for the state it is Not to believe. All civic bonds divide, Like flax fire-touched, where subjects don't believe. Away with foul impiety!

TEMPLAR.

It happens Somewhat unlucky that I want the leisure To enjoy this holy sermon. I am sent for To Saladin.

PATRIARCH.

Why then--indeed--if so -

TEMPLAR.

And will prepare the sultan, if agreeable. For your right reverend visit.

PATRIARCH.

I have heard That you found favour in the sultan's sight, I beg with all humility to be Remembered to him. I am purely motived By zeal in th' cause of God. What of too much I do, I do for him--weigh that in goodness. 'Twas then, most noble sir--what you were starting About the Jew--a problem merely!

TEMPLAR

Problem! [Goes.

PATRIARCH.

Of whose foundation I'll have nearer knowledge. Another job for brother Bonafides. Hither, my son!

[Converses with the Friar as he walks off.

SCENE--A Room in the Palace.

[SLAVES bring in a number of purses and pile them on the floor. SALADIN is present.]

SALADIN.

In troth this has no end. And is there much Of this same thing behind?

SLAVE.

   About one half.

SALADIN.

Then take the rest to Sittah. Where's Al-Hafi? What's here Al-Hafi shall take charge of straight. Or shan't I rather send it to my father; Here it slips through one's fingers. Sure in time One may grow callous; it shall now cost labour To come at much from me--at least until The treasures come from AEgypt, poverty Must shift as 't can--yet at the sepulchre The charges must go on--the Christian pilgrims Shall not go back without an alms.

SALADIN and SITTAH.

SITTAH (entering).

   Why this? Wherefore the gold to me?

SALADIN.

   Pay thyself with it, And if there's something left 'twill be in store. Are Nathan and the templar not yet come?

SITTAH.

He has been seeking for him everywhere - Look what I met with when the plate and jewels Were passing through my hands - [Showing a small portrait.

SALADIN.

   Ha! What, my brother? 'Tis he, 'tis he, WAS he, WAS he alas! Thou dear brave youth, and lost to me so early; What would I not with thee and at thy side Have undertaken? Let me have the portrait, I recollect it now again; he gave it Unto thy elder sister, to his Lilah, That morning that she would not part with him, But clasped him so in tears. It was the last Morning that he rode out; and I--I let him Ride unattended. Lilah died for grief, And never could forgive me that I let him Then ride alone. He came not back.

SITTAH.

Poor brother -

SALADIN.

Time shall be when none of us will come back, And then who knows? It is not death alone That balks the hopes of young men of his cast, Such have far other foes, and oftentimes The strongest like the weakest is o'ercome. Be as it may--I must compare this picture With our young templar, to observe how much My fancy cheated me.

SITTAH.

I therefore brought it; But give it me, I'll tell thee if 'tis like. We women see that best.

SALADIN (to a slave at the door).

Ah, who is there? The templar? let him come.

SITTAH (throws herself on a sofa apart and drops her veil).

Not to interfere, Or with my curiosity disturb you.

SALADIN.

That's right. And then his voice, will that be like? The tone of Assad's voice, sleeps somewhere yet - So -

TEMPLAR and SALADIN.

TEMPLAR.

I thy prisoner, sultan,

SALADIN.

Thou my prisoner - And shall I not to him whose life I gave Also give freedom?

TEMPLAR.

What 'twere worthy thine To do, it is my part to hear of thee, And not to take for granted. But, O Sultan, To lay loud protestations at thy feet Of gratitude for a life spared, agrees Not with my station or my character. At all times, 'tis once more, prince, at thy service.

SALADIN.

Only forbear to use it against me. Not that I grudge my enemy one pair more Of hands--but such a heart, it goes against me To yield him. I have been deceived with thee, Thou brave young man, in nothing. Yes, thou art In soul and body Assad. I could ask thee, Where then hast thou been lurking all this time? Or in what cavern slept? What Ginnistan Chose some kind Perie for thy hiding-place, That she might ever keep the flower thus fresh? Methinks I could remind thee here and yonder Of what we did together--could abuse thee For having had one secret, e'en to me - Cheat me of one adventure--yes, I could, If I saw thee alone, and not myself. Thanks that so much of this fond sweet illusion At least is true, that in my sear of life An Assad blossoms for me. Thou art willing?

TEMPLAR.

All that from thee comes to me, whatsoever It chance to prove, lies as a wish already Within my soul.

SALADIN.

We'll try the experiment. Wilt thou stay with me? dwell about me? boots not As Mussulman or Christian, in a turban Or a white mantle--I have never wished To see the same bark grow about all trees.

TEMPLAR.

Else, Saladin, thou hardly hadst become The hero that thou art, alike to all The gardener of the Lord.

SALADIN.

If thou think not The worse of me for this, we're half right.

TEMPLAR.

Quite so. One word.

SALADIN (holds out his hand).

TEMPLAR (takes it).

One man--and with this receive more Than thou canst take away again--thine wholly.

SALADIN.

'Tis for one day too great a gain--too great. Came he not with thee?

TEMPLAR.

Who?

SALADIN.

Who? Nathan.

TEMPLAR (coldly).

No, I came alone.

SALADIN.

O, what a deed of thine! And what a happiness, a blessing to thee, That such a deed was serving such a man.

TEMPLAR.

Yes, yes.

SALADIN.

So cold--no, my young friend--when God Does through our means a service, we ought not To be so cold, not out of modesty Wish to appear so cold.

TEMPLAR.

In this same world All things have many sides, and 'tis not easy To comprehend how they can fit each other.

SALADIN.

Cling ever to the best--Give praise to God, Who knows how they can fit. But, my young man, If thou wilt be so difficult, I must Be very cautious with thee, for I too Have many sides, and some of them perhaps Such as mayn't always seem to fit.

TEMPLAR.

That wounds me; Suspicion usually is not my failing.

SALADIN.

Say then of whom thou harbour'st it, of Nathan? So should thy talk imply-- canst thou suspect him? Give me the first proof of thy confidence.

TEMPLAR.

I've nothing against Nathan, I am angry With myself only.

SALADIN.

And for what?

TEMPLAR.

For dreaming That any Jew could learn to be no Jew - For dreaming it awake.

SALADIN.

Out with this dream.

TEMPLAR.

Thou know'st of Nathan's daughter, sultan. What I did for her I did--because I did it; Too proud to reap thanks which I had not sown for, I shunned from day to day her very sight. The father was far off. He comes, he hears, He seeks me, thanks me, wishes that his daughter May please me; talks to me of dawning prospects - I listen to his prate, go, see, and find A girl indeed. O, sultan, I am ashamed -

SALADIN.

A shamed that a Jew girl knew how to make Impression on thee, surely not.

TEMPLAR.

But that To this impression my rash yielding heart, Trusting the smoothness of the father's prate, Opposed no more resistance. Fool--I sprang A second time into the flame, and then I wooed, and was denied.

SALADIN.

Denied! Denied!

TEMPLAR.

The prudent father does not flatly say No to my wishes, but the prudent father Must first inquire, and look about, and think. Oh, by all means. Did not I do the same? Did not I look about and ask who 'twas While she was shrieking in the flame? Indeed, By God, 'tis something beautifully wise To be so circumspect.

SALADIN.

Come, come, forgive Something to age. His lingerings cannot last. He is not going to require of thee First to turn Jew.

TEMPLAR.

Who knows?

SALADIN.

Who? I, who know This Nathan better.

TEMPLAR.

Yet the superstition In which we have grown up, not therefore loses When we detect it, all its influence on us. Not all are free that can bemock their fetters.

SALADIN.

Maturely said--but Nathan, surely Nathan -

TEMPLAR.

The worst of superstitions is to think One's own most bearable.

SALADIN.

May be, but Nathan -

TEMPLAR.

Must Nathan be the mortal, who unshrinking Can face the moon-tide ray of truth, nor there Betray the twilight dungeon which he crawled from.

SALADIN.

Yes, Nathan is that man.

TEMPLAR.

I thought so too, But what if this picked man, this chosen sage, Were such a thorough Jew that he seeks out For Christian children to bring up as Jews - How then?

SALADIN.

Who says this of him?

TEMPLAR.

E'en the maid With whom he frets me--with the hope of whom He seemed to joy in paying me the service, Which he would not allow me to do gratis - This very maid is not his daughter--no, She is a kidnapped Christian child.

SALADIN.

Whom he Has, notwithstanding, to thy wish refused?

TEMPLAR (with vehemence).

Refused or not, I know him now. There lies The prating tolerationist unmasked - And I'll halloo upon this Jewish wolf, For all his philosophical sheep's clothing, Dogs that shall touze his hide.

SALADIN (earnestly.)

Peace, Christian!

TEMPLAR.

What! Peace, Christian--and may Jew and Mussulman Stickle for being Jew and Mussulman, And must the Christian only drop the Christian?

SALADIN (more solemnly).

Peace, Christian!

TEMPLAR (calmly.)

Yes, I feel what weight of blame Lies in that word of thine pent up. O that I knew how Assad in my place would act.

SALADIN.

He--not much better, probably as fiery. Who has already taught thee thus at once Like him to bribe me with a single word? Indeed, if all has past as thou narratest, I scarcely can discover Nathan in it. But Nathan is my friend, and of my friends

One must not bicker with the other. Bend - And be directed. Move with caution. Do not Loose on him the fanatics of thy sect. Conceal what all thy clergy would be claiming My hand to avenge upon him, with more show Of right than is my wish. Be not from spite To any Jew or Mussulman a Christian.

TEMPLAR.

Thy counsel is but on the brink of coming Somewhat too late, thanks to the patriarch's Bloodthirsty rage, whose instrument I shudder To have almost become.

SALADIN.

How! how! thou wentest Still earlier to the patriarch than to me?

TEMPLAR.

Yes, in the storm of passion, in the eddy Of indecision--pardon--oh! thou wilt No longer care, I fear, to find in me One feature of thy Assad.

SALADIN.

Yes, that fear. Methinks I know by this time from what failings Our virtue springs--this do thou cultivate, Those shall but little harm thee in my sight. But go, seek Nathan, as he sought for thee, And bring him hither: I must reconcile you. If thou art serious about the maid - Be calm, she shall be thine--Nathan shall feel That without swine's flesh one may educate A Christian child, Go. [Templar with-draws.

SITTAH (rising from the sofa).

Very strange indeed!

SALADIN.

Well, Sittah, must my Assad not have been A gallant handsome youth?

SITTAH.

If he was thus, And 'twasn't the templar who sat to the painter. But how couldst thou be so forgetful, brother, As not to ask about his parents?

SALADIN.

And Particularly too about his mother. Whether his mother e'er was in this country, That is your meaning, isn't it?

SITTAH.

You run on -

SALADIN.

Oh, nothing is more possible, for Assad 'Mong handsome Christian ladies was so welcome, To handsome Christian ladies so attached, That once a report spread--but 'tis not pleasant To bring that up. Let us be satisfied That we have got him once again--have got him With all the faults and freaks, the starts and wildness Of his warm gentle heart--Oh, Nathan must Give him the maid--Dost think so?

SITTAH.

Give--give up!

SALADIN.

Aye, for what right has Nathan with the girl If he be not her father? He who saved Her life so lately has a stronger claim To heir their rights who gave it her at first.

SITTAH.

What therefore, Saladin, if you withdraw The maid at once from the unrightful owner?

SALADIN,

There is no need of that.

SITTAH.

Need, not precisely; But female curiosity inspires Me with that counsel. There are certain men Of whom one is irresistibly impatient To know what women they can be in love with.

SALADIN.

Well then you may send for her.

SITTAH.

May I, brother?

SALADIN.

But hurt not Nathan, he must not imagine That we propose by violence to part them.

SITTAH.

Be without apprehension.

SALADIN.

Fare you well, I must make out where this Al-Hafi is.

SCENE.--The Hall in Nathan's House, as in the first scene; the things there mentioned unpacked and displayed.

DAYA and NATHAN.

DAYA.

O how magnificent, how tasty, charming - All such as only you could give--and where Was this thin silver stuff with sprigs of gold Woven? What might it cost? Yes, this is worthy To be a wedding-garment. Not a queen Could wish a handsomer.

NATHAN.

   Why wedding-garment?

DAYA.

Perhaps of that you thought not when you bought it; But Nathan, it must be so, must indeed. It seems made for a bride--the pure white ground, Emblem of innocence--the branching gold, Emblem of wealth--Now is not it delightful?

NATHAN.

What's all this ingenuity of speech for? Over whose wedding-gown are you displaying Your emblematic learning? Have you found A bridegroom?

DAYA.

   I -

NATHAN.

   Who then?

DAYA.

    I--Gracious God!

NATHAN.

Who then? Whose wedding-garment do you speak of? For this is all your own and no one's else.

DAYA.

Mine--is't for me and not for Recha?

NATHAN.

   What I brought for Recha is in another bale. Come, clear it off: away with all your rubbish.

DAYA.

You tempter--No--Were they the precious things Of the whole universe, I will not touch them Until you promise me to seize upon Such an occasion as heaven gives not twice.

NATHAN.

Seize upon what occasion? For what end?

DAYA.

There, do not act so strange. You must perceive The templar loves your Recha--Give her to him; Then will your sin, which I can hide no longer, Be at an end. The maid will come once more Among the Christians, will be once again What she was born to, will be what she was; And you, by all the benefits, for which We cannot thank you enough, will not have heaped More coals of fire upon your head.

NATHAN.

        Again Harping on the old string, new tuned indeed, But so as neither to accord nor hold.

DAYA.

How so?

NATHAN.

        The templar pleases me indeed, I'd rather he than any one had Recha; But--do have patience.

DAYA.

    Patience--and is that Not the old string you harp on?

NATHAN.

        Patience, patience, For a few days--no more. Ha! who comes here? A friar--ask what he wants.

DAYA (going).

        What can he want?

NATHAN.

Give, give before he begs. O could I tell How to come at the templar, not betraying The motive of my curiosity - For if I tell it, and if my suspicion Be groundless, I have staked the father idly. What is the matter?

DAYA (returning).

    He must speak to you.

NATHAN.

Then let him come to me. Go you meanwhile.

[Daya goes.

How gladly would I still remain my Recha's Father. And can I not remain so, though I cease to wear the name. To her, to her I still shall wear it, when she once perceives

[Friar enters.

How willingly I were so. Pious brother, What can be done to serve you?

NATHAN and FRIAR.

FRIAR.

    O not much; And yet I do rejoice to see you yet So well.

NATHAN.

    You know me then -

FRIAR.

    Who knows you not? You have impressed your name in many a hand, And it has been in mine these many years.

NATHAN (feeling for his purse).

Here, brother, I'll refresh it.

FRIAR.

    Thank you, thank you - From poorer men I'd steal--but nothing now! Only allow me to refresh my name In your remembrance; for I too may boast To mayo of old put something in your hand Not to be scorned.

NATHAN.

    Excuse me, I'm ashamed, What was it? Claim it of me sevenfold, I'm ready to atone for my forgetting.

FRIAR.

But before all, hear how this very day I was reminded of the pledge I brought you.

NATHAN.

A pledge to me intrusted?

FRIAR.

    Some time since, I dwelt as hermit on the Quarantana, Not far from Jericho, but Arab robbers Came and broke up my cell and oratory, And dragged me with them. Fortunately I Escaped, and with the patriarch sought a refuge, To beg of him some other still retreat, Where I may serve my God in solitude Until my latter end.

NATHAN.

I stand on coals - Quick, my good brother, let me know what pledge You once intrusted to me.

FRIAR.

Presently, Good Nathan, presently. The patriarch Has promised me a hermitage on Thabor, As soon as one is vacant, and meanwhile Employs me as lay-brother in the convent, And there I am at present: and I pine A hundred times a day for Thabor; for The patriarch will set me about all work, And some that I can't brook--as for example -

NATHAN

Be speedy, I beseech you.

FRIAR.

Now it happens That some one whispered in his ear to-day, There lives hard by a Jew, who educates A Christian child as his own daughter.

NATHAN (startled).

How

FRIAR.

Hear me quite out. So he commissions me, If possible to track him out this Jew: And stormed most bitterly at the misdeed; Which seems to him to be the very sin Against the Holy Ghost--That is, the sin Of all most unforgiven, most enormous; But luckily we cannot tell exactly What it consists in--All at once my conscience Was roused, and it occurred to me that I Perhaps had given occasion to this sin. Now do not you remember a knight's squire, Who eighteen years ago gave to your hands A female child a few weeks old?

NATHAN.

How that? In fact such was -

FRIAR.

Now look with heed at me, And recollect. I was the man on horseback Who brought the child.

NATHAN.

Was you?

FRIAR.

And he from whom I brought it was methinks a lord of Filnek - Leonard of Filnek.

NATHAN.

Right!

FRIAR.

Because the mother. Died a short time before; and he, the father, Had on a sudden to make off to Gazza, Where the poor helpless thing could not go with him; Therefore he sent it you--that was my message. Did not I find you out at Darun? there Consign it to you?

NATHAN.

Yes.

FRIAR.

It were no wonder My memory deceived me. I have had Many a worthy master, and this one I served not long. He fell at Askalon - But he was a kind lord.

NATHAN.

O yes, indeed; For much have I to thank him, very much - He more than once preserved me from the sword.

FRIAR.

O brave--you therefore will with double pleasure Have taken up this daughter.

NATHAN.

You have said it.

FRIAR.

Where is she then? She is not dead, I hope - I would not have her dead, dear pretty creature. If no one else know anything about it All is yet safe.

NATHAN.

Aye all!

FRIAR.

Yes, trust me, Nathan, This is my way of thinking--if the good That I propose to do is somehow twined With mischief, then I let the good alone; For we know pretty well what mischief is, But not what's for the best. 'Twas natural If you meant to bring up the Christian child Right well, that you should rear it as your own; And to have done this lovingly and truly, For such a recompense--were horrible. It might have been more prudent to have had it Brought up at second hand by some good Christian In her own faith. But your friend's orphan child You would not then have loved. Children need love, Were it the mute affection of a brute, More at that age than Christianity. There's always time enough for that--and if The maid have but grown up before your eyes With a sound frame and pious--she remains Still in her maker's eye the same. For is not Christianity all built on Judaism? Oh, it has often vexed me, cost me tears, That Christians will forget so often that Our Saviour was a Jew.

NATHAN.

You, my good brother, Shall be my advocate, when bigot hate And hard hypocrisy shall rise upon me - And for a deed--a deed--thou, thou shalt know it - But take it with thee to the tomb. As yet Has vanity ne'er tempted me to tell it To living soul--only to thee I tell it, To simple piety alone; for it Alone can feel what deeds the man who trusts In God can gain upon himself.

FRIAR.

You seem Affected, and your eye-balls swim in water.

NATHAN.

'Twas at Darun you met me with the child; But you will not have known that a few days Before, the Christians murdered every Jew in Gath, Woman and child; that among these, my wife With seven hopeful sons were found, who all Beneath my brother's roof which they had fled to, Were burnt alive.

FRIAR.

Just God!

NATHAN.

And when you came, Three nights had I in dust and ashes lain Before my God and wept--aye, and at times Arraigned my maker, raged, and cursed myself And the whole world, and to Christianity Swore unrelenting hate.

FRIAR.

Ah, I believe you.

NATHAN.

But by degrees returning reason came, She spake with gentle voice--And yet

God is, And this was his decree--now exercise What thou hast long imagined, and what surely Is not more difficult to exercise Than to imagine--if thou will it once. I rose and called out--God, I will--I will, So thou but aid my purpose--And behold You was just then dismounted, and presented To me the child wrapt in your mantle. What You said, or I, occurs not to me now - Thus much I recollect--I took the child, I bore it to my couch, I kissed it, flung Myself upon my knees and sobbed--my God, Now have I one out of the seven again!

FRIAR.

Nathan, you are a Christian! Yes, by God You are a Christian--never was a better.

NATHAN

Heaven bless us! What makes me to you a Christian Makes you to me a Jew. But let us cease To melt each other--time is nigh to act, And though a sevenfold love had bound me soon To this strange only girl, though the mere thought, That I shall lose in her my seven sons A second time distracts me--yet I will, If providence require her at my hands, Obey.

FRIAR.

The very thing I should advise you; But your good genius has forestalled my thought.

NATHAN.

The first best claimant must not seek to tear Her from me.

FRIAR.

No most surely not.

NATHAN.

And he, That has not stronger claims than I, at least Ought to have earlier.

FRIAR.

Certainly.

NATHAN.

By nature And blood conferred.

FRIAR.

I mean so too.

NATHAN.

Then name The man allied to her as brother, uncle, Or otherwise akin, and

I from him Will not withhold her--she who was created And was brought up to be of any house, Of any faith, the glory--I, I hope, That of your master and his race you knew More than myself.

FRIAR.

I hardly think that, Nathan; For I already told you that I passed A short time with him.

NATHAN.

Can you tell at least The mother's family name? She was, I think, A Stauffen.

FRIAR.

May be--yes, in fact, you're right.

NATHAN.

Conrade of Stauffen was her brother's name - He was a templar.

FRIAR.

I am clear it was. But stay, I recollect I've yet a book, 'Twas my dead lord's--I drew it from his bosom, While we were burying him at Askalon.

NATHAN.

Well!

FRIAR.

There are prayers in't, 'tis what we call A breviary. This, thought I, may yet serve Some Christian man--not me indeed, for I Can't read.

NATHAN.

No matter, to the thing.

FRIAR.

This book is written at both ends quite full, And, as I'm told, contains, in his hand-writing About both him and her what's most material.

NATHAN.

Go, run and fetch the book--'tis fortunate; I am ready with its weight in gold to pay it, And thousand thanks beside--Go, run.

FRIAR.

Most gladly; But 'tis in Arabic what he has written. [Goes.

NATHAN.

No matter--that's all one--do fetch it--Oh! If by its means I may retain the daughter, And purchase with it such a son-in-law; But that's unlikely--well, chance as it may. Who now can have been with the patriarch To tell this tale? That I must not forget To ask about. If 't were of Daya's?

NATHAN and DAYA

DAYA (anxiously breaks in).

    Nathan!

NATHAN.

Well!

DAYA.

  Only think, she was quite frightened at it, Poor child, a message -

NATHAN.

  From the patriarch?

DAYA.

   No - The sultan's sister, princess Sittah, sends.

NATHAN.

And not the patriarch?

DAYA.

  Can't you hear? The princess Has sent to see your Recha.

NATHAN.

  Sent for Recha Has Sittah sent for Recha? Well, if Sittah, And not the patriarch, sends.

DAYA.

   Why think of him?

NATHAN.

Have you heard nothing from him lately--really Seen nothing of him--whispered nothing to him?

DAYA.

How, I to him?

NATHAN.

  Where are the messengers?

DAYA.

There, just before you.

NATHAN.

I will talk with them Out of precaution. If there's nothing lurking Beneath this message of the patriarch's doing--[Goes.

DAYA.

And I--I've other fears. The only daughter, As they suppose, of such a rich, rich Jew, Would for a Mussulman be no bad thing; I bet the templar will be choused, unless I risk the second step, and to herself Discover who she is. Let me for this Employ the first short moments we're alone; And that will be--oh, as I am going with her. A serious hint upon the road I think Can't be amiss--yes, now or never--yes.

ACT V.

SCENE.--A Room in the Palace; the Purses still in a pile.

SALADIN, and, soon after, several MAMALUKES.

SALADIN (as he comes in).

Here lies the money still, and no one finds The dervis yet--he's probably got somewhere Over a chess-board. Play would often make The man forget himself, and why not, me. Patience--Ha! what's the matter.

SALADIN and IBRAHIM.

IBRAHIM.

     Happy news - Joy, sultan, joy, the caravan from Cairo Is safe arrived and brings the seven years' tribute Of the rich Nile.

SALADIN.

    Bravo, my Ibrahim, Thou always wast a welcome messenger, And now at length--at length--accept my thanks For the good tidings.

IBRAHIM (waiting).

  Hither with them, sultan.

SALADIN.

What art thou waiting for? Go.

IBRAHIM.

    Nothing further For my glad news?

SALADIN.

  What further?

IBRAHIM.

    Errand boys Earn hire--and when their message smiles i' the telling, The sender's hire by the receiver's bounty Is oft outweighed. Am I to be the first Whom

Saladin at length has learnt to pay In words? The first about whose recompense The sultan higgled?

SALADIN.

  Go, pick up a purse.

IBRAHIM.

No, not now--you might give them all away

SALADIN.

All--hold, man. Here, come hither, take these two - And is he really going-- shall he conquer Me then in generosity? for surely 'Tis harder for this fellow to re- fuse Than 'tis for me to give. Here, Ibrahim - Shall I be tempted, just before my exit, To be a different man--small Saladin Not die like Saladin, then wherefore live so?

ABDALLAH and SALADIN.

ABDALLAH.

Hail, Sultan!

SALADIN.

  If thou comest to inform me That the whole convoy is arrived from Egypt, I know it already.

ABDALLAH.

  Do I come too late?

SALADIN.

Too late, and why too late? There for thy tidings Pick up a purse or two.

ABDALLAH.

   Does that make three?

SALADIN.

So thou wouldst reckon--well, well, take them, take them.

ABDALLAH.

A third will yet be here if he be able.

SALADIN.

How so?

ABDALLAH.

  He may perhaps have broke his neck. We three, as soon as certain of the com- ing Of the rich caravan, each crossed our horses, And galloped hitherward. The foremost fell, Then I was foremost, and continued so Into the city, but sly Ibrahim,

Who knows the streets -

SALADIN.

But he that fell, go, seek him.

ABDALLAH.

That will I quickly--if he lives, the half Of what I've got is his. [Goes.

SALADIN.

What a fine fellow! And who can boast such mamalukes as these; And is it not allowed me to imagine That my example helped to form them. Hence With the vile thought at last to turn another.

A third COURIER.

Sultan -

SALADIN.

Was't thou who fell?

COURIER.

No, I've to tell thee That Emir Mansor, who conducts the convoy, Alights.

SALADIN.

O bring him to me--Ah, he's there - Be welcome, Emir. What has happened to thee? For we have long expected thee.

SALADIN and EMIR.

EMIR (after the wont obeisance).

This letter Will show, that, in Thebais, discontents Required thy Abulkassem's sabred hand, Ere we could march. Since that, our progress, sultan, My zeal has sped most anxiously.

SALADIN.

I trust thee - But my good Mansor take without delay - Thou art not loth to go further--fresh protection, And with the treasure on to Libanon; The greater part at least I have to lodge With my old father.

EMIR.

O, most willingly.

SALADIN.

And take not a slight escort. Libanon Is far from quiet, as thou wilt have heard; The templars stir afresh, be therefore cautious. Come, I must see thy troop, and give the orders.

[To a slave.
Say I shall be with Sittah when I've finished.

SCENE--A Place of Palms.

The TEMPLAR walking to and fro.
TEMPLAR.
Into this house I go not--sure at last He'll show himself--once, once they used to see me So instantly, so gladly--time will come When he'll send out most civilly to beg me Not to pace up and down before his door. Psha--and yet I'm a little nettled too; And what has thus embittered me against him? He answered yes. He has refused me nothing As yet. And Saladin has undertaken To bring him round. And does the Christian nestle Deeper in me than the Jew lurks in him? Who, who can justly estimate himself? How comes it else that I should grudge him so The little booty that he took such pains To rob the Christians of? A theft, no less Than such a creature tho'--but whose, whose creature? Sure not the slave's who floated the mere block On to life's barren strand, and then ran off; But his the artist's, whose fine fancy moulded Upon the unowned block a godlike form, Whose chisel graved it there. Recha's true father, Spite of the Christian who begot her, is, Must ever be, the Jew. Alas, were I To fancy her a simple Christian wench, And without all that which the Jew has given, Which only such a Jew could have bestowed - Speak out my heart, what had she that would please thee? No, nothing! Little! For her very smile Shrinks to a pretty twisting of the muscles - Be that, which makes her smile, supposed unworthy Of all the charms in ambush on her lips? No, not her very smile--I've seen sweet smiles Spent on conceit, on foppery, on slander, On flatterers, on wicked wooers spent, And did they charm me then? then wake the wish To flutter out a life beneath their sunshine? Indeed not--Yet I'm angry with the man Who alone gave this higher value to her. How this, and why? Do I deserve the taunt With which I was dismissed by Saladin? 'Tis bad enough that Saladin should think so; How little, how contemptible must I Then have appeared to him--all for a girl. Conrade, this will not do--back, back--And if Daya to boot had prated matter to me Not easy to be proved--At last he's coming, Engaged in earnest converse--and with whom? My friar in Nathan's house! then he knows all - Perhaps has to the pa-

triarch been betrayed. O Conrade, what vile mischiefs thou hast brooded Out of thy cross-grained head, that thus one spark Of that same passion, love, can set so much O' 'th' brain in flame? Quick, then, determine, wretch, What shalt thou say or do? Step back a moment And see if this good friar will please to quit him.

NATHAN and the FRIAR come together out of Nathan's house.

NATHAN.

Once more, good brother, thanks.

FRIAR.

    The like to you.

NATHAN.

To me, and why; because I'm obstinate - Would force upon you what you have no use for?

FRIAR.

The book besides was none of mine. Indeed It must at any rate belong to th' daughter; It is her whole, her only patrimony - Save she has you. God grant you ne'er have reason To sorrow for the much you've done for her.

NATHAN.

How should I? that can never be; fear nothing.

FRIAR.

Patriarchs and templars -

NATHAN,

    Have not in their power Evil enough to make me e'er repent. And then--But are you really well assured It is a templar who eggs on your patriarch?

FRIAR.

It scarcely can be other, for a templar Talked with him just before, and what I heard Agreed with this.

NATHAN.

    But there is only one Now in Jerusalem; and him I know; He is my friend, a noble open youth.

FRIAR.

The same. But what one is at heart, and what One gets to be in active life, mayn't always Square well together.

NATHAN.

No, alas, they do not. Therefore unangered I let others do Their best or worst. O brother, with your book I set all at defiance, and am going Straight with it to the Sultan.

FRIAR.

God be with you! Here I shall take my leave.

NATHAN.

And have not seen her - Come soon, come often to us. If to-day The patriarch make out nothing--but no matter, Tell him it all to-day, or when you will.

FRIAR.

Not I--farewell!

NATHAN.

Do not forget us, brother My God, why may I not beneath thy sky Here drop upon my knees; now the twined knot, Which has so often made my thinkings anxious, Untangles of itself--God, how I am eased, Now that I've nothing in the world remaining That I need hide--now that I can as freely Walk before man as before thee, who only Need'st not to judge a creature by his deeds - Deeds which so seldom are his own--O God!

NATHAN and TEMPLAR.

TEMPLAR (coming forward).

Hoa, Nathan, take me with you.

NATHAN.

Ha! Who calls? Is it you, knight? And whither have you been That you could not be met with at the Sultan's?

TEMPLAR.

We missed each other--take it not amiss.

NATHAN.

I, no, but Saladin.

TEMPLAR.

You was just gone.

NATHAN.

O, then you spoke with him; I'm satisfied.

TEMPLAR.

Yes--but he wants to talk with us together.

NATHAN.

So much the better. Come with me, my step Was eitherwise bent thither.

TEMPLAR.

May I ask, Nathan, who 'twas now left you?

NATHAN.

Did you know him?

TEMPLAR.

Was't that good-hearted creature the lay-brother, Whom the hoar patriarch has a knack of using To feel his way out?

NATHAN.

That may be. In fact He's at the patriarch's.

TEMPLAR.

'Tis no awkward hit To make simplicity the harbinger Of craft.

NATHAN.

If the simplicity of dunces, But if of honest piety?

TEMPLAR.

This last No patriarch can believe in.

NATHAN.

I'll be bound for't This last belongs to him who quitted me. He'll not assist his patriarch to accomplish A vile or cruel purpose.

TEMPLAR.

Such, at least, He would appear--but has he told you then Something of me?

NATHAN.

Of you? No--not by name, He can't well be acquainted with your name.

TEMPLAR.

No, that not.

NATHAN.

He indeed spoke of a templar, Who -

TEMPLAR.

What?

NATHAN.

But by this templar could not mean To point out you.

TEMPLAR.

Stay, stay, who knows? Let's hear.
NATHAN.
Who has accused me to his patriarch.
TEMPLAR.
Accused thee, no, that by his leave is false. Nathan do hear me--I am not the
man Who would deny a single of his actions; What I have done, I did. Nor am I
one Who would defend all he has done as right - Why be ashamed of failing? Am
I not Firmly resolved on better future conduct? And am I not aware how much the
man That's willing can improve? O, hear me, Nathan - I am the templar your lay-
brother talked of - Who has accused--You know what made me angry, What set
the blood in all my veins on fire, The mad-cap that I was--I had drawn nigh To fling
myself with soul and body whole Into your arms--and you received me, Nathan--
How cold, how lukewarm, for that's worse than cold. - How with words weighed
and measured, you took care To put me off; and with what questioning About my
parentage, and God knows what, You seemed to answer me--I must not think on't
If I would keep my temper--Hear me, Nathan - While in this ferment--Daya steps
behind me, Bolts out a secret in my ear, which seemed At once to lend a clue to
your behaviour.
NATHAN.
How so?
TEMPLAR.
 Do hear me to the end. I fancied That what you from the Christians had
purloined You wasn't content to let a Christian have; And so the project struck me
short and good, To hold the knife to your throat till -
NATHAN.
 Short and good; And good--but where's the good?
TEMPLAR.
 Yet hear me, Nathan, I own I did not right--you are unguilty, No doubt. The
prating Daya does not know What she reported--has a grudge against you - Seeks to
involve you in an ugly business - May be, may be, and I'm a crazy looby, A credu-
lous enthusiast--both ways mad - Doing ever much too much, or much too little
- That too may be--forgive me, Nathan.
NATHAN.

If Such be the light in which you view -

TEMPLAR.

In short I to the patriarch went. I named you not. That, as I said, was false. I only stated In general terms, the case, to learn his notion, That too might have been let alone--assuredly. For knew I not the patriarch then to be A knave? And might I not have talked with you? And ought I to have exposed the poor girl--ha! To part with such a father? Now what happens? The patriarch's villainy consistent ever Restored me to myself--O, hear me out - Suppose he was to ferret out your name, What then? What then? He cannot seize the maid, Unless she still belong to none but you. 'Tis from your house alone that he could drag her Into a convent; therefore grant her me - Grant her to me, and let him come. By God - Sever my wife from me--he'll not be rash Enough to think about it. Give her to me, Be she or no thy daughter, Christian, Jewess, Or neither, 'tis all one, all one--I'll never In my whole life ask of thee which she is, Be't as it may.

NATHAN.

You may perhaps imagine That I've an interest to conceal the truth.

TEMPLAR.

Be't as it may.

NATHAN.

I neither have to you Nor any one, whom it behooved to know it, Denied that she's a Christian, and no more Than my adopted daughter. Why, to her I have not yet betrayed it--I am bound To justify only to her.

TEMPLAR.

Of that Shall be no need. Indulge, indulge her with Never beholding you with other eyes - Spare, spare her the discovery. As yet You have her to yourself, and may bestow her; Give her to me--oh, I beseech thee, Nathan, Give her to me, I, only I can save her A second time, and will.

NATHAN.

Yes, could have saved her. But 'tis all over now--it is too late.

TEMPLAR.

How so, too late.

NATHAN.

Thanks to the patriarch.

TEMPLAR.

How Thanks to the patriarch, and for what? Can he Earn thanks of us. For what?

NATHAN.

That now we know To whom she is related--to whose hands She may with confidence be now delivered.

TEMPLAR.

He thank him who has more to thank him for.

NATHAN.

From theirs you now have to obtain her, not From mine.

TEMPLAR.

Poor Recha--what befalls thee? Oh, Poor Recha--what had been to other orphans A blessing, is to thee a curse. But, Nathan, Where are they, these new kinsmen?

NATHAN.

Where they are?

TEMPLAR.

Who are they?

NATHAN.

Who--a brother is found out To whom you must address yourself.

TEMPLAR.

A brother! And what is he, a soldier or a priest? Let's hear what I've to hope.

NATHAN.

As I believe He's neither of the two--or both. Just now I cannot say exactly.

TEMPLAR.

And besides He's -

NATHAN.

A brave fellow, and with whom my Recha Will not be badly placed.

TEMPLAR.

But he's a Christian. At times I know not what to make of you - Take it not ill of me, good Nathan. Will she Not have to play the Christian among Christians;

And when she has been long enough the actress Not turn so? Will the tares in time not stifle The pure wheat of your setting--and does that Affect you not a whit--you yet declare She'll not be badly placed.

NATHAN.

I think, I hope so. And should she there have need of any thing Has she not you and me?

TEMPLAR.

Need at her brother's - What should she need when there? Won't he provide His dear new sister with all sorts of dresses, With comfits and with toys and glittering jewels? And what needs any sister wish for else - Only a husband? And he comes in time. A brother will know how to furnish that, The Christianer the better. Nathan, Nathan, O what an angel you had formed, and how Others will mar it now!

NATHAN.

Be not so downcast, Believe me he will ever keep himself Worthy our love.

TEMPLAR.

No, say not that of mine. My love allows of no refusal--none. Were it the merest trifle--but a name. Hold there--has she as yet the least suspicion Of what is going forward?

NATHAN.

That may be, And yet I know not whence.

TEMPLAR.

It matters not, She shall, she must in either case from me First learn what fate is threatening. My fixed purpose To see her not again, nor speak to her, Till I might call her mine, is gone. I hasten -

NATHAN.

Stay, whither would you go?

TEMPLAR.

To her, to learn If this girl's soul be masculine enough To form the only resolution worthy Herself.

NATHAN.

What resolution?

TEMPLAR.

    This--to ask No more about her brother and her father, And -

NATHAN.

    And -

TEMPLAR.

    To follow me. E'en if she were So doing to become a Moslem's wife.

NATHAN.

Stay, you'll not find her--she is now with Sittah, The Sultan's sister.

TEMPLAR.

    How long since, and wherefore?

NATHAN.

And would you there behold her brother, come Thither with me.

TEMPLAR.

    Her brother, whose then? Sittah's Or Recha's do you mean?

NATHAN.

Both, both, perchance. Come this way--I beseech you, come with me. [Leads off the Templar with him.

SCENE.--The Sultan's Palace. A Room in Sittah's Apartment.

SITTAH and RECHA.

SITTAH.

How I am pleased with thee, sweet girl! But do Shake off this perturbation, be not anxious, Be not alarmed, I want to hear thee talk - Be cheerful.

RECHA.

    Princess!

SITTAH.

    No, not princess, child. Call me thy friend, or Sittah, or thy sister, Or rather aunt, for I might well be thine; So young, so good, so prudent, so much knowledge, You must have read a great deal to be thus.

RECHA.

I read--you're laughing, Sittah, at your sister, I scarce can read.

SITTAH.

Scarce can, you little fibber.

RECHA.

My father's hand or so--I thought you spoke Of books.

SITTAH.

Aye, surely so I did, of books.

RECHA.

Well really now it puzzles me to read them.

SITTAH.

In earnest?

RECHA.

Yes, in earnest, for my father Hates cold book-learning, which makes an impression With its dead letters only on the brain.

SITTAH.

What say you? Aye, he's not unright in that. So then the greater part of what you know -

RECHA.

I know but from his mouth--of most of it I could relate to you, the how, the where, The why he taught it me.

SITTAH.

So it clings closer, And the whole soul drinks in th' instruction.

RECHA.

Yes, And Sittah certainly has not read much.

SITTAH.

How so? Not that I'm vain of having read; But what can be thy reason? Speak out boldly, Thy reason for it.

RECHA.

She is so right down, Unartificial--only like herself And books do seldom leave us so; my father Says.

SITTAH.

What a man thy father is, my Recha.

RECHA.

Is not he?

SITTAH.

How he always hits the mark.
RECHA.
Does not he? And this father -
SITTAH.
Love, what ails thee?
RECHA.
This father -
SITTAH.
God, thou'rt weeping
RECHA.
And this father - It must have vent, my heart wants room, wants room.
SITTAH.
Child, child, what ails you, Recha?
RECHA.
And this father I am to lose.
SITTAH.
Thou lose him, O no, never: Arise, be calm, how so? It must not be.
RECHA.
So shall thy offer not have been in vain, To be my friend, my sister.
SITTAH.
Maid, I am. Rise then, or I must call for help.
RECHA.
Forgive, My agony made me awhile forgetful With whom I am. Tears, sobbing, and despair, Can not avail with Sittah. Cool calm reason Alone is over her omnipotent; Whose cause that pleads before her, he has conquered.
SITTAH.
Well, then!
RECHA.
My friend, my sister, suffer not Another father to be forced upon me.
SITTAH.
Another father to be forced upon thee - Who can do that, or wish to do it, Recha?
RECHA.

Who? Why my good, my evil genius, Daya, She, she can wish it, will it--and can do it. You do not know this dear good evil Daya. God, God forgive it her--reward her for it; So much good she has done me, so much evil.

SITTAH.

Evil to thee--much goodness she can't have.

RECHA.

O yes, she has indeed.

SITTAH.

  Who is she?

RECHA.

    Who? A Christian, who took care of all my childhood. You cannot think how little she allowed me To miss a mother--God reward her for it - But then she has so teased, so tortured me.

SITTAH.

And about what? Why, how, when?

RECHA.

    The poor woman, I tell thee, is a Christian--and she must From love torment--is one of those enthusiasts Who think they only know the one true road To God.

SITTAH.

  I comprehend thee.

RECHA.

    And who feel Themselves in duty bound to point it out To every one who is not in this path, To lead, to drag them into it. And indeed They can't do otherwise consistently; For if theirs really be the only road On which 'tis safe to travel--they cannot With comfort see their friends upon another Which leads to ruin, to eternal ruin: Else were it possible at the same instant To love and hate the same man. Nor is 't this Which forces me to be aloud complainant. Her groans, her prayers, her warnings, and her threats, I willingly should have abided longer - Most willingly--they always called up thoughts Useful and good; and whom does it not flatter To be by whomsoever held so dear, So precious, that they cannot bear the thought Of parting with us at some time for ever?

SITTAH.

Most true.
RECHA.

   But--but--at last this goes too far; I've nothing to oppose to it, neither patience, Neither reflection--nothing.
SITTAH.

   How, to what?
RECHA.

To what she has just now, as she will have it, Discovered to me.
SITTAH.

   How discovered to thee?
RECHA.

Yes, just this instant. Coming hitherward We past a fallen temple of the Christians - She all at once stood still, seemed inly struggling, Turned her moist eyes to heaven, and then on me. Come, says she finally, let us to the right Thro' this old fane--she leads the way, I follow. My eyes with horror overran the dim And tottering ruin--all at once she stops By the sunk steps of a low Moorish altar. - O how I felt, when there, with streaming tears And wringing hands, prostrate before my feet She fell
SITTAH.

   Good child -
RECHA.

   And by the holy Virgin, Who there had hearkened many a prayer, and wrought Many a wonder, she conjured, intreated, With looks of heartfelt sympathy and love, I would at length take pity of myself - At least forgive, if she must now unfold What claims her church had on me.
SITTAH.

   Ah! I guessed it.
RECHA.

That I am sprung of Christian blood--baptised - Not Nathan's daughter--and he not my father. God, God, he not my father! Sittah, Sittah, See me once more low at thy feet.
SITTAH.

   O Recha, Not so; arise, my brother's coming, rise.

SALADIN, SITTAH, and RECHA.
SALADIN (entering).
What is the matter, Sittah?
SITTAH.
  She is swooned-- God -
SALADIN.
 Who?
SITTAH.
  You know sure.
SALADIN.
  What, our Nathan's daughter? What ails her?
SITTAH.
 Child, come to thyself, the sultan.
RECHA.
No, I'll not rise, not rise, not look upon The Sultan's countenance--I'll not ad-
mire The bright reflection of eternal justice And mercy on his brow, and in his eye,
Before -
SALADIN.
 Rise, rise.
RECHA.
  Before he shall have promised -
SALADIN.
Come, come, I promise whatsoe'er thy prayer.
RECHA.
Nor more nor less than leave my father to me, And me to him. As yet I can-
not tell What other wants to be my father. Who Can want it, care I not to inquire.
Does blood Alone then make the father? blood alone?
SALADIN (raising her).
Who was so cruel in thy breast to shed This wild suspicion? Is it proved, made
clear?
RECHA.
It must, for Daya had it from my nurse, Whose dying lips intrusted it to her.
SALADIN.

Dying, perhaps delirious; if 'twere true, Blood only does not make by much the father, Scarcely the father of a brute, scarce gives The first right to endeavour at deserving The name of father. If there be two fathers At strife for thee, quit both, and take a third, And take me for thy father.

SITTAH.

  Do it, do it.

SALADIN.

I will be a kind father--but methinks A better thought occurs, what hast thou need Of father upon father? They will die, So that 'tis better to look out by times For one that starts fair, and stakes life with life On equal terms. Knowst thou none such?

SITTAH.

  My brother, Don't make her blush.

SALADIN.

Why that was half my project. Blushing so well becomes the ugly, that The fair it must make charming--I have ordered Thy father Nathan hither, and another, Dost guess who 'tis? one other.--Sittah, you Will not object?

SITTAH.

  Brother -

SALADIN.

  And when he comes, Sweet girl, then blush to crimson.

RECHA.

  Before whom - Blush?

SALADIN.

   Little hypocrite--or else grow pale, Just as thou willst and canst. Already there?

SITTAH (to a female slave who comes in).

Well, be they ushered in. Brother, 'tis they.

SALADIN, SITTAH, RECHA, NATHAN, and TEMPLAR.

SALADIN.

Welcome, my dear good friends. Nathan, to you I've first to mention, you may send and fetch Your monies when you will.

NATHAN.

Sultan -
SALADIN.

And now I'm at your service.
NATHAN.

Sultan -
SALADIN.

For my treasures Are all arrived. The caravan is safe. I'm richer than I've been these many years. Now tell me what you wish for, to achieve Some splendid speculation--you in trade Like us, have never too much ready cash.
NATHAN (going towards Recha).

Why first about this trifle?--I behold An eye in tears, which 'tis far more important To me to dry. My Recha thou hast wept, What hast thou lost? Thou art still, I trust, my daughter.
RECHA.

My father!
NATHAN.

That's enough, we are understood By one another; but be calm, be cheerful. If else thy heart be yet thy own--if else No threatened loss thy trembling bosom wring Thy father shall remain to thee.
RECHA.

None, none.
TEMPLAR.

None, none--then I'm deceived. What we don't fear To lose, we never fancied, never wished Ourselves possessed of. But 'tis well, 'tis well. Nathan, this changes all--all. Saladin, At thy command we came, but I misled thee, Trouble thyself no further.
SALADIN.

Always headlong; Young man, must every will then bow to thine, Interpret all thy meanings?
TEMPLAR.

Thou hast heard, Sultan, hast seen.
SALADIN.

Aye, 'twas a little awkward Not to be certain of thy cause.

TEMPLAR.

I now Do know my doom,

SALADIN.

Pride in an act of service Revokes the benefit. What thou hast saved Is therefore not thy own, or else the robber, Urged by his avarice thro' fire-crumbling halls, Were like thyself a hero. Come, sweet maid,

[Advances toward Recha in order to lead her up to the Templar.

Come, stickle not for niceties with him. Other--he were less warm and proud, and had Paused, and not saved thee. Balance then the one Against the other, and put him to the blush, Do what he should have done--own thou thy love - Make him thy offer, and if he refuse, Or o'er forgot how infinitely more By this thou do for him than he for thee - What, what in fact has he then done for thee But make himself a little sooty? That (Else he has nothing of my Assad in him, But only wears his mask) that was mere sport, Come, lovely girl.

SITTAH.

Go, go, my love, this step Is for thy gratitude too short, too trifling.

[They are each taking one of Recha's hands when Nathan with a solemn gesture of prohibition says,

NATHAN.

Hold, Saladin--hold, Sittah.

SALADIN.

Ha! thou too?

NATHAN.

One other has to speak.

SALADIN.

Who denies that? Unquestionably, Nathan, there belongs A vote to such a foster-father--and The first, if you require it. You perceive I know how all the matter lies.

NATHAN.

Not all-- I speak not of myself. There is another, A very different man, whom, Saladin, I must first talk with.

SALADIN.

Who?

NATHAN.

Her brother.

SALADIN.

Recha's?

NATHAN.

Yes, her's.

RECHA.

My brother--have I then a brother?

[The templar starts from his silent and sullen inattention.

TEMPLAR.

Where is this brother? Not yet here? 'Twas here I was to find him.

NATHAN.

Patience yet a while.

TEMPLAR (very bitterly).

He has imposed a father on the girl, He'll find her up a brother.

SALADIN.

That was wanting! Christian, this mean suspicion ne'er had past The lips of Assad. Go but on -

NATHAN.

Forgive him, I can forgive him readily. Who knows What in his place, and at his time of life, We might have thought ourselves? Suspicion, knight,

[Approaching the templar in a friendly manner.

Succeeds soon to mistrust. Had you at first Favoured me with your real name.

TEMPLAR.

How? what?

NATHAN.

You are no Stauffen.

TEMPLAR.

Who then am I? Speak.

NATHAN.

Conrade of Stauffen is no name of yours.

TEMPLAR.

What is my name then?

NATHAN.

  Guy of Filnek.

TEMPLAR.

  How?

NATHAN.

You startle -

TEMPLAR.

  And with reason. Who says that?

NATHAN.

I, who can tell you more. Meanwhile, observe I do not tax you with a falsehood.

TEMPLAR.

  No?

NATHAN.

May be you with propriety can wear Yon name as well.

TEMPLAR.

  I think so too. (God--God Put that speech on his tongue.)

NATHAN.

  In fact your mother - She was a Stauffen: and her brother's name, (The uncle to whose care you were resigned, When by the rigour of the climate chased, Your parents quitted Germany to seek This land once more) was Conrade. He perhaps Adopted you as his own son and heir. Is it long since you hither travelled with him? Is he alive yet?

TEMPLAR.

  So in fact it stands. What shall I say? Yes, Nathan, 'tis all right: Tho' he himself is dead. I came to Syria With the last reinforcement of our order, But--but what has all this long tale to do With Recha's brother, whom -

NATHAN.

  Your father -

TEMPLAR.

  Him, Him did you know?

NATHAN.

He was my friend.

TEMPLAR.

    Your friend? And is that possible?

NATHAN.

  He called himself Leonard of Filnek, but he was no German.

TEMPLAR.

You know that too?

NATHAN.

  He had espoused a German, And followed for a time your mother thither.

TEMPLAR.

No more I beg of you--But Recha's brother -

NATHAN.

Art thou

TEMPLAR.

  I, I her brother -

RECHA.

    He, my brother?

SITTAH.

So near akin -

RECHA (offers to clasp him).

  My brother!

TEMPLAR (steps back).

    Brother to her -

RECHA (turning to Nathan).

It cannot be, his heart knows nothing of it. We are deceivers, God.

SALADIN (to the templar).

    Deceivers, yes; All is deceit in thee, face, voice, walk, gesture, Nothing belongs to thee. How, not acknowledge A sister such as she? Go.

TEMPLAR (modestly approaching him).

    Sultan, Sultan O do not misinterpret my amazement - Thou never saw'st in such a moment, prince, Thy Assad's heart--mistake not him and me.

[Hastening towards Nathan.

O Nathan, you have taken, you have given, Both with full hands indeed; and now--yes--yes, You give me more than you have taken from me, Yes, infinitely more--my sister--sister.

[Embraces Recha.

NATHAN.

Blanda of Filnek.

TEMPLAR.

    Blanda, ha! not Recha, Your Recha now no longer--you resign her, Give her her Christian name again, and then For my sake turn her off. Why Nathan, Nathan, Why must she suffer for it? she for me?

NATHAN.

What mean you? O my children, both my children - For sure my daughter's brother is my child, So soon as he but will it!

[While they embrace Nathan by turns, Saladin draws nigh to Sittah.

SALADIN.

    What sayst thou Sittah to this?

SITTAH.

    I'm deeply moved.

SALADIN.

    And I Half tremble at the thought of the emotion Still greater, still to come. Nathan, a word

[While he converses with Nathan, Sittah goes to express her sympathy to the others.

With thee apart. Wast thou not saying also That her own father was no German born? What was he then? Whence was he?

NATHAN.

    He himself Never intrusted me with that. From him I knew it not.

SALADIN.

You say he was no Frank?

NATHAN.

No, that he owned: he loved to talk the Persian.

SALADIN.

The Persian--need I more? 'Tis he--'twas he!

NATHAN.

Who?

SALADIN.

Assad certainly, my brother Assad.

NATHAN.

If thou thyself perceive it, be assured; Look in this book--[Gives the breviary.

SALADIN (eagerly looking.)

O 'tis his hand, his hand, I recollect it well.

NATHAN.

They know it not; It rests with thee what they shall learn of this.

SALADIN (turning over the breviary.)

I not acknowledge my own brother's children, Not own my nephew--not my children--I Leave them to thee? Yes, Sittah, it is they, [Aloud. They are my brother's and thy brother's children. [Rushes to embrace them.

SITTAH.

What do I hear? Could it be otherwise? [The like.

SALADIN (to the templar).

Now, proud boy, thou shalt love me, thou must love me,

[To Recha.

And I am, what I offered to become, With or without thy leave.

SITTAH.

I too--I too.

SALADIN (to the templar.)

My son--my Assad--my lost Assad's son.

TEMPLAR.

I of thy blood--then those were more than dreams With which they used to lull my infancy - Much more.

[Falls at the Sultan's feet.

SALADIN (raising him.)

Now mark his malice. Something of it He knew, yet would have let me butcher him - Boy, boy!

[During the silent continuance of reciprocal embraces the curtain falls.]

The Codes Of Hammurabi And Moses
W. W. Davies

QTY

The discovery of the Hammurabi Code is one of the greatest achievements of archaeology, and is of paramount interest, not only to the student of the Bible, but also to all those interested in ancient history...

Religion   **ISBN:** *1-59462-338-4*   **Pages:132**
MSRP $12.95

The Theory of Moral Sentiments
Adam Smith

QTY

This work from 1749. contains original theories of conscience amd moral judgment and it is the foundation for systemof morals.

Philosophy   **ISBN:** *1-59462-777-0*   **Pages:536**
MSRP $19.95

Jessica's First Prayer
Hesba Stretton

QTY

In a screened and secluded corner of one of the many railway-bridges which span the streets of London there could be seen a few years ago, from five o'clock every morning until half past eight, a tidily set-out coffee-stall, consisting of a trestle and board, upon which stood two large tin cans, with a small fire of charcoal burning under each so as to keep the coffee boiling during the early hours of the morning when the work-people were thronging into the city on their way to their daily toil...

Childrens   **ISBN:** *1-59462-373-2*   **Pages:84**
MSRP $9.95

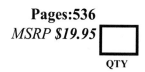

My Life and Work
Henry Ford

QTY

Henry Ford revolutionized the world with his implementation of mass production for the Model T automobile. Gain valuable business insight into his life and work with his own auto-biography... "We have only started on our development of our country we have not as yet, with all our talk of wonderful progress, done more than scratch the surface. The progress has been wonderful enough but..."

Biographies/   **ISBN:** *1-59462-198-5*   **Pages:300**
MSRP $21.95

The Art of Cross-Examination
Francis Wellman

QTY

I presume it is the experience of every author, after his first book is published upon an important subject, to be almost overwhelmed with a wealth of ideas and illustrations which could readily have been included in his book, and which to his own mind, at least, seem to make a second edition inevitable. Such certainly was the case with me; and when the first edition had reached its sixth impression in five months, I rejoiced to learn that it seemed to my publishers that the book had met with a sufficiently favorable reception to justify a second and considerably enlarged edition. ..

Reference   ISBN: *1-59462-647-2*

Pages:412

MSRP $19.95

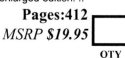

On the Duty of Civil Disobedience
Henry David Thoreau

QTY

Thoreau wrote his famous essay, On the Duty of Civil Disobedience, as a protest against an unjust but popular war and the immoral but popular institution of slave-owning. He did more than write—he declined to pay his taxes, and was hauled off to gaol in consequence. Who can say how much this refusal of his hastened the end of the war and of slavery ?

Law   ISBN: *1-59462-747-9*

Pages:48

MSRP $7.45

Dream Psychology Psychoanalysis for Beginners
Sigmund Freud

QTY

Sigmund Freud, born Sigismund Schlomo Freud (May 6, 1856 - September 23, 1939), was a Jewish-Austrian neurologist and psychiatrist who co-founded the psychoanalytic school of psychology. Freud is best known for his theories of the unconscious mind, especially involving the mechanism of repression; his redefinition of sexual desire as mobile and directed towards a wide variety of objects; and his therapeutic techniques, especially his understanding of transference in the therapeutic relationship and the presumed value of dreams as sources of insight into unconscious desires.

Psychology   ISBN: *1-59462-905-6*

Pages:196

MSRP $15.45

The Miracle of Right Thought
Orison Swett Marden

QTY

Believe with all of your heart that you will do what you were made to do. When the mind has once formed the habit of holding cheerful, happy, prosperous pictures, it will not be easy to form the opposite habit. It does not matter how improbable or how far away this realization may see, or how dark the prospects may be, if we visualize them as best we can, as vividly as possible, hold tenaciously to them and vigorously struggle to attain them, they will gradually become actualized, realized in the life. But a desire, a longing without endeavor, a yearning abandoned or held indifferently will vanish without realization.

Self Help   ISBN: *1-59462-644-8*

Pages:360

MSRP $25.45

QTY

☐ **The Rosicrucian Cosmo-Conception Mystic Christianity** *by Max Heindel* ISBN: *1-59462-188-8* **$38.95**
The Rosicrucian Cosmo-conception is not dogmatic, neither does it appeal to any other authority than the reason of the student. It is: not controversial, but is: sent forth in the, hope that it may help to clear.. New Age/Religion Pages 646

☐ **Abandonment To Divine Providence** *by Jean-Pierre de Caussade* ISBN: *1-59462-228-0* **$25.95**
"The Rev. Jean Pierre de Caussade was one of the most remarkable spiritual writers of the Society of Jesus in France in the 18th Century. His death took place at Toulouse in 1751. His works have gone through many editions and have been republished... Inspirational/Religion Pages 400

☐ **Mental Chemistry** *by Charles Haanel* ISBN: *1-59462-192-6* **$23.95**
Mental Chemistry allows the change of material conditions by combining and appropriately utilizing the power of the mind. Much like applied chemistry creates something new and unique out of careful combinations of chemicals the mastery of mental chemistry... New Age Pages 354

☐ **The Letters of Robert Browning and Elizabeth Barret Barrett 1845-1846 vol II** ISBN: *1-59462-193-4* **$35.95**
by Robert Browning and Elizabeth Barrett Biographies Pages 596

☐ **Gleanings In Genesis (volume I)** *by Arthur W. Pink* ISBN: *1-59462-130-6* **$27.45**
Appropriately has Genesis been termed "the seed plot of the Bible" for in it we have, in germ form, almost all of the great doctrines which are afterwards fully developed in the books of Scripture which follow... Religion/Inspirational Pages 420

☐ **The Master Key** *by L. W. de Laurence* ISBN: *1-59462-001-6* **$30.95**
In no branch of human knowledge has there been a more lively increase of the spirit of research during the past few years than in the study of Psychology, Concentration and Mental Discipline. The requests for authentic lessons in Thought Control, Mental Discipline and... New Age/Business Pages 422

☐ **The Lesser Key Of Solomon Goetia** *by L. W. de Laurence* ISBN: *1-59462-092-X* **$9.95**
This translation of the first book of the "Lernegton" which is now for the first time made accessible to students of Talismanic Magic was done, after careful collation and edition, from numerous Ancient Manuscripts in Hebrew, Latin, and French.. New Age/Occult Pages 92

☐ **Rubaiyat Of Omar Khayyam** *by Edward Fitzgerald* ISBN:*1-59462-332-5* **$13.95**
Edward Fitzgerald, whom the world has already learned, in spite of his own efforts to remain within the shadow of anonymity, to look upon as one of the rarest poets of the century, was born at Bredfield, in Suffolk, on the 31st of March, 1809. He was the third son of John Purcell... Music Pages 172

☐ **Ancient Law** *by Henry Maine* ISBN: *1-59462-128-4* **$29.95**
The chief object of the following pages is to indicate some of the earliest ideas of mankind, as they are reflected in Ancient Law, and to point out the relation of those ideas to modern thought. Religion/History Pages 452

☐ **Far-Away Stories** *by William J. Locke* ISBN: *1-59462-129-2* **$19.45**
"Good wine needs no bush, but a collection of mixed vintages does. And this book is just such a collection. Some of the stories I do not want to remain buried for ever in the museum files of dead magazine-numbers an author's not unpardonable vanity..." Fiction Pages 272

☐ **Life of David Crockett** *by David Crockett* ISBN: *1-59462-250-7* **$27.45**
"Colonel David Crockett was one of the most remarkable men of the times in which he lived. Born in humble life, but gifted with a strong will, an indomitable courage, and unremitting perseverance.. Biographies/New Age Pages 424

☐ **Lip-Reading** *by Edward Nitchie* ISBN: *1-59462-206-X* **$25.95**
Edward B. Nitchie, founder of the New York School for the Hard of Hearing, now the Nitchie School of Lip-Reading, Inc, wrote "LIP-READING Principles and Practice". The development and perfecting of this meritorious work on lip-reading was an undertaking... How-to Pages 400

☐ **A Handbook of Suggestive Therapeutics, Applied Hypnotism, Psychic Science** ISBN: *1-59462-214-0* **$24.95**
by Henry Munro Health/New Age/Health/Self-help Pages 376

☐ **A Doll's House: and Two Other Plays** *by Henrik Ibsen* ISBN: *1-59462-112-8* **$19.95**
Henrik Ibsen created this classic when in revolutionary 1848 Rome. Introducing some striking concepts in playwriting for the realist genre, this play has been studied the world over. Fiction/Classics/Plays 308

☐ **The Light of Asia** *by sir Edwin Arnold* ISBN: *1-59462-204-3* **$13.95**
In this poetic masterpiece, Edwin Arnold describes the life and teachings of Buddha. The man who was to become known as Buddha to the world was born as Prince Gautama of India but he rejected the worldly riches and abandoned the reigns of power when... Religion/History/Biographies Pages 170

☐ **The Complete Works of Guy de Maupassant** *by Guy de Maupassant* ISBN: *1-59462-157-8* **$16.95**
"For days and days, nights and nights, I had dreamed of that first kiss which was to consecrate our engagement, and I knew not on what spot I should put my lips..." Fiction/Classics Pages 240

☐ **The Art of Cross-Examination** *by Francis L. Wellman* ISBN: *1-59462-309-0* **$26.95**
Written by a renowned trial lawyer, Wellman imparts his experience and uses case studies to explain how to use psychology to extract desired information through questioning. How-to/Science/Reference Pages 408

☐ **Answered or Unanswered?** *by Louisa Vaughan* ISBN: *1-59462-248-5* **$10.95**
Miracles of Faith in China Religion Pages 112

☐ **The Edinburgh Lectures on Mental Science (1909)** *by Thomas* ISBN: *1-59462-008-3* **$11.95**
This book contains the substance of a course of lectures recently given by the writer in the Queen Street Hall, Edinburgh. Its purpose is to indicate the Natural Principles governing the relation between Mental Action and Material Conditions... New Age/Psychology Pages 148

☐ **Ayesha** *by H. Rider Haggard* ISBN: *1-59462-301-5* **$24.95**
Verily and indeed it is the unexpected that happens! Probably if there was one person upon the earth from whom the Editor of this, and of a certain previous history, did not expect to hear again... Classics Pages 380

☐ **Ayala's Angel** *by Anthony Trollope* ISBN: *1-59462-352-X* **$29.95**
The two girls were both pretty, but Lucy who was twenty-one who supposed to be simple and comparatively unattractive, whereas Ayala was credited, as her Bombwhat romantic name might show, with poetic charm and a taste for romance. Ayala when her father died was nineteen... Fiction Pages 484

☐ **The American Commonwealth** *by James Bryce* ISBN: *1-59462-286-8* **$34.45**
An interpretation of American democratic political theory. It examines political mechanics and society from the perspective of Scotsman James Bryce Politics Pages 572

☐ **Stories of the Pilgrims** *by Margaret P. Pumphrey* ISBN: *1-59462-116-0* **$17.95**
This book explores pilgrims religious oppression in England as well as their escape to Holland and eventual crossing to America on the Mayflower, and their early days in New England... History Pages 268

QTY

The Fasting Cure *by Sinclair Upton* **ISBN:** *1-59462-222-1* **$13.95**
In the Cosmopolitan Magazine for May, 1910, and in the Contemporary Review (London) for April, 1910, I published an article dealing with my experiences in fasting. I have written a great many magazine articles, but never one which attracted so much attention... New Age/Self Help/Health Pages 164 ☐

Hebrew Astrology *by Sepharial* **ISBN:** *1-59462-308-2* **$13.45**
In these days of advanced thinking it is a matter of common observation that we have left many of the old landmarks behind and that we are now pressing forward to greater heights and to a wider horizon than that which represented the mind-content of our progenitors... Astrology Pages 144 ☐

Thought Vibration or The Law of Attraction in the Thought World **ISBN:** *1-59462-127-6* **$12.95**
by William Walker Atkinson Psychology/Religion Pages 144 ☐

Optimism *by Helen Keller* **ISBN:** *1-59462-108-X* **$15.95**
Helen Keller was blind, deaf, and mute since 19 months old, yet famously learned how to overcome these handicaps, communicate with the world, and spread her lectures promoting optimism. An inspiring read for everyone... Biographies/Inspirational Pages 84 ☐

Sara Crewe *by Frances Burnett* **ISBN:** *1-59462-360-0* **$9.45**
In the first place, Miss Minchin lived in London. Her home was a large, dull, tall one, in a large, dull square, where all the houses were alike, and all the sparrows were alike, and where all the door-knockers made the same heavy sound... Childrens/Classic Pages 88 ☐

The Autobiography of Benjamin Franklin *by Benjamin Franklin* **ISBN:** *1-59462-135-7* **$24.95**
The Autobiography of Benjamin Franklin has probably been more extensively read than any other American historical work, and no other book of its kind has had such ups and downs of fortune. Franklin lived for many years in England, where he was agent... Biographies/History Pages 332 ☐

Name	
Email	
Telephone	
Address	
City, State ZIP	

☐ **Credit Card** ☐ **Check / Money Order**

Credit Card Number	
Expiration Date	
Signature	

Please Mail to: Book Jungle
PO Box 2226
Champaign, IL 61825
or Fax to: 630-214-0564

ORDERING INFORMATION

web*: www.bookjungle.com*
email*: sales@bookjungle.com*
fax*: 630-214-0564*
mail*: Book Jungle PO Box 2226 Champaign, IL 61825*
or PayPal *to sales@bookjungle.com*

Please contact us for bulk discounts

DIRECT-ORDER TERMS

**20% Discount if You Order
Two or More Books**
Free Domestic Shipping!
Accepted: Master Card, Visa,
Discover, American Express